HOW MAKING A SANDWICH CAN CHANGE YOUR WORLD

Jeff Lichtenstein

Publisher, Copyright, and Additional Information

How Making a s Sandwich Can Change Your World

by Jeff Lichtenstein

Published by PB&J STRATEGY, LLC

505 Cocoplum Dr S, Jupiter, Florida, 33458

Jeff@PBJStrategy.com

ISBN- 979-8-218-24988-5 (Paperback)

979-8-218-25254-0 (Hardback)

Editing by Lisa Howard

Cover design and interior design by CoverKitchen

Cover photography by Wrigley McDevitt Photography

Have you ever awakened one morning to the sight of your home, your neighbors' homes, and your entire community wiped off the face of the Earth?

Unless you've had that experience yourself, you can't imagine what happened to the residents of Lee County and Fort Myers, Florida.

Contents

Contents

Foreword
from Jeff Lobb

I have a bunch of family: I'm a proud dad of six. That's right, six! Five boys and one girl. My wife is the captain of our ship. She runs and powers the domain of our life and household.

Both at work and in everyday life, I'm a coach at heart—I coach kids' football and lacrosse, I'm president of the lacrosse league, and I'm president of the board of education for our elementary school system. Last year, we helped Johnny, one of our 8th-grade lacrosse players, as he battled leukemia. The lacrosse league created stickers for kids' helmets to support Johnny, we made shirts, we arranged visits to his home, we had kids FaceTime him daily after practices, and we helped raise money for his and his family's care.

An extraordinary thing happened as we did all of this: we won a lot of games, ultimately only losing by only one point in the finals. We played together more, communicated better, and had a purpose.

Granted, our story is not a unique one. Winston Churchill said, "We make a living by what we get; we make a life by what we give." That likely explains why when there's a good cause, people rally around it. We organically want to help. Time and time again, helping others brings out the best of us. We saw exactly that scenario happen when the league helped Johnny.

When *I* was a kid, I lived in a very blue-collar neighborhood in Elizabeth, New Jersey. We had a small row house with no backyard, and three of us shared one bedroom. The street was our domain.

I started my first sales job at age 10. Even though I didn't think of it as sales at the time, in reality, stacking fruit and setting up an open-air fruit market at 4 a.m. on Saturdays was the start of learning the art of sales. By 9 a.m., I was shouting "Oranges, eight for a $1!" or "Golden apples for sale!" I learned early on how to deal with people, money, and the responsibility of showing up.

At the ripe old age of 19—during my junior year of college—I was getting my real estate license. However, just before that career kicked off, the person who worked at the real estate company I was about to join said I'd be great in sales and told me that his brother-in-law could use my help on his radio show.

I was intrigued! I interviewed for the job and got hired. Off I went, selling ad time on a radio show about tourism. It was an amazing opportunity—I got great experience in learning the craft of how to connect with people. But then Desert Storm happened and we had to part ways.

That brought me back to my career in real estate. The most magical lesson I received came early on in my career and was imparted by my mentor and broker Joe Budrow. He said to me,

"Look at the agents at the front desk! They're waiting for the phone to ring to get business. I want you to go out and find business instead of waiting for it." My reply was, "Well, that makes sense, because what if the phone doesn't ring? Then they don't get any business." He just smiled.

Now, after having spent 36 years in real estate as an agent, owner of brokerages, and an executive for several companies with 30,000 agents and 800 offices, I've learned a lot about the business of sales. Here's the truth: it really isn't about the company, it's about the *people*. The *people* are always the true assets of a company.

I've also had the pleasure of being a coach and advisor to many agents, companies, and leaders throughout the country. I deliver keynotes and mastermind workshops on sales, marketing, and business strategies internationally. All of this experience has led to a deep understanding of what it takes to make people and businesses truly succeed, and it's also led me to meet some amazing people.

I met Jeff Lichtenstein a little over six years ago, when I was speaking at a national conference. Jeff is the owner and founder of Echo Fine Properties, an agency of some 80 realtors. Do you know that feeling when you meet someone and you feel like they just have that "it" factor? "It" is an energy, a personality, a certain magnetism.

As soon as I met Jeff, I knew he had that "it." He's a natural leader. When people like Jeff want more out of themselves and their business, they seek like-minded individuals and mentors who can help them level up.

Jeff and I had an immediate connection. We wound up working weekly together on strategy, rebranding, systems, and sales growth. Then I watched Jeff go through stage 3 kidney cancer. He set an example of how to research thoroughly, move quickly, and act with urgency, all while having a positive outlook, remaining calm, and taking care of his business and family. Then and ever since, he has led his team and company through many different markets and challenges, including the challenges of rebranding his company and doing business during a worldwide pandemic.

Even though change is a daily variable, not everyone is good at dealing with change. Jeff is—he's someone who can not only pivot quickly but can also execute strategies faster than most! Sometimes when people do what they do best so naturally, that inherently creates its own story, sometimes an unforgettable story. This book tells one such story.

On September 28, 2022, Hurricane Ian made landfall, devastating parts of the western coast of Florida. So many lives were impacted, changed, and even lost; many areas were completely devastated.

In the face of this destruction and chaos, Jeff and his team took action. Although they didn't know what the end result would be or what kind of risks they would need to take, they knew they had to help. They knew they had to deliver aid and deliver that aid quickly, so they pushed aside their own personal lives and business matters to help people on the West Coast. They sacrificed their time and money to help people through a national tragedy.

The results of their efforts turned out to be the very definition of culture, branding, and leadership, and their efforts went further than they'd imagined. In that sense, their situation was comparable to what happened to our lacrosse team when we helped Johnny and then went on a winning streak.

The story you're about to read—the story of what Echo did for the community and the community did for Echo—not only had an impact on many people, it also showcased many of the most valuable lessons about people and businesses today. The successes you're about to read about led to business strategies and actionable ideas that all of us must analyze and apply to the world of corporate America and the world of start-ups and entrepreneurs. These concepts raise questions that challenge the status quo and explore the value of a successful culture and why people are the main asset of any company. Jeff and his team have found the formula to engaging in scheduled and organic giving, the kind of giving that changes businesses and lives. In short, if your company needs to rethink its strategy, rethink its culture, or rethink its sales and marketing strategy, *The PB&J Strategy* is a must-read.

I'm so proud to be associated with Jeff Lichtenstein, Echo Fine Properties, and their team for helping their community on such a deep level all while embodying the core principles of business success. And they did so via one of my favorite foods of all time: peanut-butter-and-jelly sandwiches! PB&Js rekindle so many memories from my childhood, memories I cherish despite having grown up during challenging times.

You might be wondering, "How on Earth do PB&Js relate *at all* to business or sales or building community?"

I'll leave that mystery for you to solve as you read the Echo team's weird, inspiring, and remarkable story. I'll just say this: their tale will allow you to discover principles that can change your business and your world.

Enjoy the read, take great notes, and execute with purpose!

Preface

On September 28th, 2022, winds at speeds of 150 mph hit the outer islands of Fort Myers. Ever since modern recordkeeping started in 1851, Ian was in the Top Five!

The cyclone grew rapidly in the Gulf of Mexico and was predicted to land in the Tampa Bay area. My daughter Jade drove South from Tallahassee to our home in Jupiter. (In Tallahassee, the storm could have been a Category 2 or 3.) All schools in the state of Florida were closed that week. But rather than striking Tampa Bay, the storm made a last-minute turn that kept it South of Tampa and at the very southern part of the cone. Captiva Island, Sanibel Island, Pine Island, and the entire Fort Myers area were devastated as many people were caught off guard and did not evacuate.

Hurricane Ian cut a chunk of the Sanibel Causeway off and into the ocean, disconnecting the bridge from the main inland islands of Fort Myers. Almost 4.5 million families lost power, including over 3 million in Florida. Entire towns were under water and destroyed. Ian ended up being the costliest storm in the history of Florida, eventually causing over $112 billion in damages and more than 150 deaths directly or indirectly, according to the National Oceanic and Atmospheric Administration (NOAA). Before Ian dissipated on October 1st, the hurricane also impacted Georgia, Virginia, the Carolinas, and Cuba.

Fort Myers is three hours away from where our real estate brokerage, Echo Fine Properties, is located. Many of us have connections to the West Coast and vacation there. I watched that evening as Ian was destroying communities I knew so well. Then the majestic Sanibel Causeway which I've driven many times to Sanibel and Capita Islands broke off into the San Carlos Bay! Cutting off people from the mainland made my heart just... drop. The day after the storm hit, several of us wanted to get involved and help the affected communities. After all, these folks were our neighbors—we had to do something! And quickly!

In just five days, we came up with an idea, a website, t-shirts, stickers, set-up materials, a product distribution plan, guidelines, and marketing and public relations plans. We made 1,926 peanut butter sandwiches and then put a crew together to deliver them to people in need. I thought, "If we can do that, what else can we do to make a big difference in our community, our business, and our lives?" You might be asking the same thing about your own community, business, and life.

And so this is the story of how a little 80-person brokerage made and delivered 25,000 peanut-butter-and-jelly sandwiches (with a children's recipe!) in a short period of time. Not only did this action make a big difference, it also garnered unexpected gifts for us and our business. Along with the gratitude of our neighbors, we received priceless amounts of free publicity, business opportunities, collaborations, implementations, innovations, and positive energy. In short, (and strictly in business terms) we generated an estimated and unanticipated half-million-dollar publicity return on our investment.

The lessons of the PB&J Strategy should be deployed not only in instances of disaster but scheduled in the regular course of each calendar year. The PB&J Strategy should be learned and implemented by anyone in sales and business and by human resources departments.

So, if you want to be inspired to not only help people but also get out of an idea rut and change your personal and business life, keep reading! The true story you're about to read includes a step-by-step breakdown of how we recognized a problem, established our goals, and accomplished what we set out to do.

This process applies to all areas of business. It will change not only your business but your world!

Jeff Lichtenstein

Dedicated to
my Grandpa Gerry

My Grandpa Gerry was a sayings guy. "Keep it simple" is inscribed on his tombstone. "You can't make a purse out of sow's ear" was another of his favorites. *My* favorite has always been "You can't do a good deal with a bad guy." That's why whenever I build up our organization, I look for good guys—men and women with good character who are empathic and who strive for win-win situations. When you seek out those people, I've found there's better synergy, teamwork, positive energy, and collaboration. Focusing on having those "good guy" people also limits gossip, negativity, and stagnation, and having givers on the team also builds forward momentum and leads to doing more business. The more you give, the more you get! Which my Grandpa also used to say.

The Value of a PB&J Sandwich

Purple and gold:
Colors of royalty.
Peanut butter & jelly:
A meal fit for kings and queens?
Certainly for a child;
Certainly for a chef;
Certainly for those in need.
And certainly for the memories of yesteryear.
Smell, sight, and touch embedded in us—
Friends, joy, and love radiate.
Yes, a meal fit for kings and queens.

Chapter 1:
The Zoom Call

On Thursday, September 29th, 2022, the day after Hurricane Ian decimated Florida's West Coast, twenty of our real estate agents organized a Zoom call to try to figure out what we could do to help. Captiva Island, Sanibel, and the Fort Myers area are our neighbors to the west. Our company name of Echo was even conceived in Captiva Island! Sara, one of our key people, had her wedding date planned there; I've often vacationed there. Helping our West Coast neighbors was *personal*.

Some of us remembered wanting to help when Katrina had hit New Orleans years before. (I'd gotten talked out of it by people who said things like "It's a mess" and "There really isn't much you can do.") Other people outside of our company wanted to help with Ian, too. Feelings and emotions were raw. As the leader of our group, I felt that if we were going to do something, it needed to happen while the iron of emotion was hot. Brainstorming began.

The lead idea was to help a family in Port Charlotte that owned a pizza restaurant. Let them cook, and we'd bring supplies—from clothing to diapers to food—and throw a block party. Bringing "home" to "home," so to speak.

But I didn't love the idea since the supplies we'd be bringing went far past food—it felt a bit all over the place. I was trying to find something that could involve the community with one idea. However, the family at the restaurant was elated when we brought it up and the wife started to cry.

I melted when I heard that. We were all in.

Chapter 2:
The Follow-Up
Zoom Call

On Monday, October 3rd, we got on a Zoom follow-up call. The family backed out! They had a one-year-old child, and the mom was too stressed to participate. I was totally frustrated. Not at the family—their reaction was completely understandable—but because we hadn't developed a good Plan B. It was suggested that we still carry out our plans for the family, but in late November. That was all fine and good, but as Chef Andrés from World Central Kitchen would have pointed out, the urgency of now didn't mean acting in November.

Ideas we'd thought of before varied wildly, from holding toy drives to donating dog food to raising money. But if people wanted to give money, the Red Cross or World Central Kitchen would have fulfilled that need—no one was going to give money to a real estate organization to distribute. We're not a charity, and setting up the paperwork to become one would have meant taking on a whole different level of responsibility.

I abruptly ended the meeting. We had too many voices in the kitchen on the call; I decided to figure this out with help of small groups.

Chapter 3:
Picking Up
the Peanut Shells

Sometimes groupthink is great, but other times it can lead to confusion and hinder decision-making. In this case, we needed one voice. Since I had already taken in lots of good input from the group, I decided to set some rules:

1.   Organically, the group wants to do something good for the right reasons.
2.   It's a one-thought idea.
3.   It's something we can all get behind.
4.   It's something the community can get behind.
5.   It utilizes our database and the strength of the community.
6.   It associates us personally and as an organization with what we're doing. The campaign resonates and sticks.
7.   We own the concept.
8.   It's a win for the cause and a win for the business.

That was quite a list... Not so easy to fulfill!

Chapter 4:
The Pivot to PB&J

Helping the restaurant was out. Supplying used clothing, tools, and pet food were some other ideas we explored. I thought used clothing was a good idea because it checked a lot of the boxes: it was a one-thought idea, and to do it, we could really reach out to the community and use our database.

So I reached out to an old *Mad Men*-style advertiser whose services I use and who's an excellent writer. I asked him to create a punchy tagline and call to action. He came up with "Empty your closet and fill a neighbor's heart: send your threads to your West Coast neighbors."

I liked it, but then we hit a new major drawback: finding outlets for used clothing is harder than you'd think. We were back at square one (again). Tools can be dangerous to handle, and we weren't sure what to bring or request from the community. Pet food was being handled by specific pet rescue operations.

My rule was that if we didn't have a 100% useful idea, we should reboot. Fortunately, that was when my marketing whiz told me a story about a guy name Lou Farrell who had started a charity in Philadelphia during the pandemic. It was called Operation Bread Drop, and the organizers made peanut-butter-and-jelly sandwiches. They did so because when the pandemic first hit, restaurants shut down. Restaurants are a key source of food for the homeless. Suddenly, there was a massive and urgent need to get food to this already half-forgotten population.

Lou came from the restaurant industry himself. Having supervised a soup kitchen for years, he understood the severity and necessity of the situation. He figured that if he talked to people who cared, maybe they could make food specifically for homeless individuals.

Lou settled on PB&J sandwiches as the product of choice. For one thing, people could make the sandwiches in their homes during lockdowns. They had all the time in the world to make the sandwiches, and the sandwiches could be easily distributed. Not only that, people know what to do with PB&Js: eat one sandwich now and stick the other sandwich in their pocket for lunch later.

Lou spent a massive amount of time and money on his program. He recently passed the mark of 300,000 sandwiches given away to the homeless! He also guided and advised me as we crafted our own campaign. Lou wasn't trying to market any kind of service, nor did he have an organization. He wasn't interested in team building. But like us, Lou was highly motivated to solve a problem.

Unlike us, Lou asked other people to make the sandwiches. (One older couple, he told me, consistently knocked out 100 sandwiches every week while watching *60 Minutes*.) Lou eventually figured out how much he needed and didn't need and then put together distribution networks rather than handing out sandwiches individually. He learned how to pack the sandwiches standing up and had a whole host of other tips that he passed along to us.

Chapter 5:
Why PB&J Works

Maybe it sounds silly, but hear me out: making those PB&J sandwiches was *really* smart. I liked the idea immediately. For starters, Lou had provided a test case that proved the idea worked, and he had clearly showed all the reasons *why* it worked. It's like buying into a franchise—once you see it work in one market, a huge degree of risk has been removed from the equation. Lou gave me all the ingredients that made Operation Bread Drop successful:

- Each sandwich provides 450 essential calories.
- This is not a five-star meal—no artisan bread is needed.
- It's comfort food that's comfortable.
- It lasts.
- It travels.
- It's easy to make.
- It's fun to make, from how it smells to how it looks and tastes.

- It's understandable—consumers know what to do with it.

Exercise:
Foolproofing an Idea

When we embarked upon our PB&J campaign, we knew our idea stood a better chance because we knew that Lou's similar idea was already working. Lou was using it to deal with a pandemic-induced catastrophe, but the fact that there was already a partial working blueprint with proven results removed a lot of risk for us. In the same vein, when we wanted to get into commercial real estate and title insurance and when we wanted to expand our footprint into Martin County and Southern Palm Beach County, we had similar had-sort-of-done-it-already advantages.

- Our existing agents had clients who were looking for commercial property.
- Our new residential leads were sometimes also looking for commercial property.
- Both commercial real estate and title insurance were related businesses to what we were already doing.
- Our existing agents oftentimes recommended how to handle title insurance.
- We didn't need to buy office space.
- We were already familiar with working with joint venture partners.

- Our website people had worked on commercial websites before, so we had the knowledge we needed to launch a commercial real estate endeavor.
- Going in, we already knew the players in the industry, which minimized our risk.
- Our agents in Northern Palm Beach Country were already searching for properties, plus we were already generating buyer and seller inquiries.
- We'd won Best Real Estate Brokerage for Palm Beach County and the State of Florida. We could obviously leverage those awards.
- Echo was already a known entity—we popped up high in online rankings for the area and we already had the connections we needed in the press to get extra coverage.
- We already had systems in place internally to handle the new business ventures. That eased the cost of breaking into those businesses.

Now It's Your Turn!

What new endeavor are you thinking of doing? It could be something as simple as launching a new marketing plan or as big as an expanding into a new business area. What will minimize your risks? What risks do you face?

Chapter 6:
Core Group

Before presenting this new plan to our entire team, I told two key people in our company what we were going to do. The first was our social media director. Like Lou, he's from Philly. We could have been delivering tiddlywinks—if the idea had originated in Philly, Rob would have been sold. Besides, he seriously liked the idea off the bat. Our administrator Sara had doubts, but she and I had built up enough trust over the years that she got behind the idea with blind faith. If Sara hadn't believed in my idea and trusted me, our endeavor wouldn't have happened. It says a lot about your people when they can move forward with an idea even if they don't fully like or understand it.

Chapter 7: Our Basic Marketing Plan

After talking to my two key players, I wrote out a basic marketing plan covering what we needed to get started:

- An email to our group explaining what this was about and why.
- A website.
- A tagline.
- A logo.
- Stickers to hand out.
- How we were going to make the sandwiches.
- Who we were going to distribute them to.
- How to get the community involved.

The tagline we used was "Coming together—sticking together." "Coming together" was something the community was doing, and "sticking together" showed that we were sticking by our neighbors and each other. It was also a great wordplay on

PB&J. We came up with so many phrases: " Let's jam!" "Sticky situation." "Spread the word!" And lots more.

We debated using Lou's Bread Drop logo, but ultimately, that logo didn't say anything about PB&J. I thought we needed our effort to be laser-focused, so I had a logo made that incorporated love, PB&J, purple and gold colors, and the campaign URL. The logo also needed to look a bit homemade and at the same time not silly. The final products were going to a good cause, after all, but it was the community who'd be making the sandwiches.

"Sticking together" was the bigger part of the tagline, so we decided to use that in the URL. We used our own website to host the page but purchased the domain name www.PBJStickingTogether.com (which redirected to www.echofineproperties.com/ pbj/). I figured it was inappropriate to advertise our website as the place to visit, plus our Echo URL was also less memorable. I even had our web people remove lots of real estate info normally on the pages so that this particular page could be dedicated solely to the cause and not show any homes or other real estate links. After all, the main impulse that had generated this effort wasn't business—it was disaster relief.

Next up was the sticker. A sticker was important because we needed something tangible to give out. When people vote, they proudly put a sticker on their shirt, and this would be the same thing. Bonus: stickers were cheap. We rushed them in for the people who volunteered and later ended up putting the stickers on all of the sandwiches. We found that the recipients liked seeing them because they showed where the sandwiches had come from.

Another bonus: people who put the stickers on had fun sticking them. (Who doesn't love stickers?) And it was also an unexpected business win for us because of the branding—the press wound up loving shooting the sandwiches with the stickers on them as a visual. One television producer from a show I went on was a sandwich-maker during our effort and later emailed me wanting more stickers to give to all those who had helped.

Sara got on the phone and found no shortage of places who wanted sandwiches. She picked three different spots for our first delivery: a food pantry in Harlem Heights, a church in

Fort Myers, and a makeshift distribution center on Pine Island (which had been hit the hardest). But that said, getting into the mass PB&J sandwich business involved lots more work than we had imagined.

While the ingredients are obvious—peanut butter, grape jelly, and white bread—you also need knives, spoons, tables, tin foil to make the sandwiches on, gloves of various sizes, Ziploc® bags, hairnets, coolers, and storage containers. Plus we needed to learn the subtleties of making sandwiches and how to get our team and the community involved.

See the PB&J Website

Chapter 8:
They Think I'm Nuts

The next issue was convincing our group of 80 people that we were going to make PB&Js. If I hadn't been a proven leader and the boss—both things needed to be in place—it would have been harder to make things happen. At first, I got a lot of stares and people saying nothing, but my confidence and excitement were contagious. One by one, people started coming in with supplies.

Chris Burke came in carrying loaves of Wonder Bread in both hands. Craig the Leg brought in Peter Pan peanut butter and Welch's jelly. Tasha became a master of asking and getting stores to donate. Everyone was running around with supplies. It looked a bit weird—the office was getting cluttered and starting to smell like Wonder Bread. But a funny thing happened: it was fun! People were smiling.

Our PR company loved what we were doing and pitched it to one of the local news outlets. Everyone wanted to cover it. *Everyone!* Local NBC, CBS, FOX, and ABC stations wanted the story. NBC and FOX each wanted to come out on the following Tuesday morning as we made sandwiches. We had already planned our first internal sandwich-making session for Friday morning.

But late on Thursday, I got word that ABC wanted to cover us later in the day. I sent out an email to the team saying that if anyone wanted to switch times or come in then, they could. We ended up with a bigger-than-expected turnout on Friday morning. And yet another surprise: the laughter and fun was overwhelming as we figured out how to get gobs of peanut butter out of jars and onto bread. Peter Pan, Jif®, Skippy®, Publix... all of those brands brought back memories. The same with the jelly varieties, Smucker's® and Welch's—everyone had their favorites.

Plastic clear knives breaking, calls for long spoons, learning how to spread better, not too much jelly... Putting peanut butter on both sides as a base so the sandwich wouldn't get wet (we later made a how-to video about this for the website) and stacking sandwiches up *juuuust* so tall so that they wouldn't get smooshed were things we learned along the way.

From left to right...Craig Heger, Andrew Seifter, Phineas Wish, Tasha Guerino

Exercise: Storytelling and Selling Ideas Internally

Selling a campaign or even a new procedure internally isn't easy! Often, fear of what your own team might think of it and their potential backlash will kill good ideas because management doesn't want to deal with the potential negativity.

The first part of selling an idea is relating it to your audience indirectly. You might think that the purpose/outcome would be the most important aspect of the idea, but people often balk when it comes to change, even if there's an obvious solution and being stubborn and not accepting it just makes no sense. Let me share an example from our office.

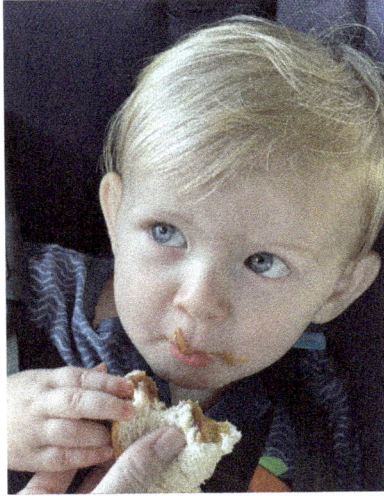

Brooks Harper. Quality Control

Lately, we've had a terrible time with internal communications and getting tasks done. We have 80 people in our organization, and oftentimes, one hand doesn't know what the other is doing. Communicating by email wasn't working anymore—our rapid growth meant we couldn't just communicate one-on-one without letting everybody on the team know what we were all doing. (Lots of companies have this issue.) One of our administrators said, "Hey, let's not reinvent the wheel! Let's just start with something easy, something we're already using." That something was a program called Basecamp. A few of us were already using it, but our photographer, videographer, brochure writer, and agents weren't.

Mayor Chelsea Reed in Peanut Butter Gold

I sent out an email to everybody (except for the agents) saying that we were *all* going to use Basecamp. Moans and groans ensued. I then used an indirect story of *why* we needed to use it rather just saying "It's going to benefit us": I gave an example of a restaurant owner taking all of the orders, cooking all of the food, serving all of the food, taking all of the checks, washing all of the dishes, and cleaning everything up. Maybe that works if the restaurant only has a few tables, but as it expands, the restaurant owner would have no chance of succeeding. "That's where we are today," I said. People related to that.

After that, I made some individual calls and listened to each person's fears. Then we made a decision that *yes,* we were going to do this. We started by getting all of our staff on board, including the agents. Our administrator and our IT person were already using Basecamp and had already presented it to the staff. One of the keys was not only using the app but understanding the need to schedule each task, with time-blocking in the morning being the most essential function we needed to utilize. (Basecamp is great for keeping everything in one place.)

Then we talked to everyone about how things were going. At first our photographer was overwhelmed, but once he started talking through things, what had initially looked overwhelming wasn't. Then when I talked to him about another change, he started telling me how Basecamp was already the answer and it was the best thing we'd ever done.

Mount PB&J

From left to right... Dara Dickinson, Jeff, Suzanne Slate,
Mayor Chelsea Reed, Reporter Derek Lowe

Now It's Your Turn!

1. Name one internal problem within your organization.

2. Do you have a solution? What is it?

3. What resistance to the solution might you encounter?

4. What steps do you need to take to implement the solution?

5. When will you get started?

Chapter 9:
Press, Crust, Debate and Repeat 1,926 Times

Someone wanted to throw out the crust. But I love the crust! I still remember reaching all the way to the back of the loaf to grab the crust when I was a kid. Thinking about crust made me realize that we were *all* remembering being a kid.

Our agent Chris Burke is a dead ringer for Will Ferrell. When I was talking with him, someone brought that up and prompted me to remember something else: we'd done a charity event a few years back called The Tug of War to Stop Cancer. All of the agents had become crazy characters who led their tug-of-war teams and made funny videos about their methods. (It was kinda like those silly WWE wrestling videos.) Chris had dressed up as the Wonder Bread Man from the movie *Talladega Nights*. He said he'd put on that outfit again, this time for the news crews, so we found it in storage for him.

We ended our first morning PB&J session at noon. Then I got on the phone and called everyone to get to the office by 4 p.m. to be in time for the ABC crew. I was afraid we would have burnout, but surprisingly, we had a giant crowd and maybe 30 people making PB&Js. Our internal staff loved doing this! It was a zoo and also a major hit.

We ended that afternoon with 1,926 PB&J sandwiches between what we'd made and drop-offs from people we had talked to about making sandwiches. Then the magic happened!

Chapter 10:
A Sense of Urgency

Oftentimes, there's a limited window of time to make an impact—usually there's an urgent need, and if you don't fulfill that need when the problem is at hand, then the time has passed for both helping people and maximizing the business opportunities that go hand in hand with helping.

Looking back now, it dawns on me that it would normally have taken six months (speaking optimistically) to do what we wanted to accomplish. Accomplishing what we did in five days was flat-out heroic. The amount of arranging and dealing with obstacles was a *big* elephant, yet within a mere five days, we'd become a major firm in the field of manufacturing and distributing PB&Js. This speaks to the power of instilling everyone with the "urgency of now."

Chapter 11:
Getting the Essentials

We continued to need materials to make our sandwiches. Fortunately, to my surprise, lots of grocery stores donated to us. Many of our agents bought supplies, too. Bread was the big issue; I purchased something like $1,600 of Wonder Bread.

People had fun finding the ingredients and donating. Later on—once we'd gotten the word out—lots of people started to come in and donate ingredients. I also found out that if the volunteers who were making the sandwiches brought in the ingredients themselves, the sandwich-making became more fun and they were more invested in it. For them, going out and buying the product was part of the joy of giving.

Exercise:
The Logic of Delegation

People don't know how to delegate and often refuse to try doing it. For many, giving up the simplest of tasks is a challenge. "Nobody does it as well as I do," they say. But that attitude ends up either limiting their income or eventually spurring burnout. A lot of that "Nobody else can do it" mindset stems from control, while some people fear working with others. Mostly, though, people aren't even aware of *what* to delegate or *how* to delegate.

At Echo, we faced a delegation issue when we wanted our agents to put their bios on our website and in our printed material within two weeks of them starting with us. Ditto for the agent bio videos. Our photojournalist Rob Moore was originally tasked with writing their bios, scripting their video bios, and then filming their video bios. The problem was that he got busy and the agents weren't turning in their written questionnaire answers to kick off the overall process. Then the agents got busy with business matters. After six months, we had maybe 20% of the video bios. Nobody ever knew what to say or where to film. Eventually, though, we overcame this roadblock by delegating tasks. Here's an example of how we did that.

1. Identify something to delegate. It can be something personal or something business-related.

We wanted to get agents' bio write-ups, their profile lifestyle shots, and their profile videos done within four weeks of agents joining Echo.

2. Define the problem.

The agents, photographer, and videographer could never seem to get together.

3. Who can we delegate this issue to?

Sara Morey quarterbacked our onboarding, so it made the most sense to assign her this task since she always had first contact with incoming agents.

4. How can the person assigned to this task get the task done?

Sara created a shared calendar and now just books the dates for everyone. We time-block every Friday as a day to tackle this task. We approached a new builder about holding our photo shoots and video sessions at their models, and they said yes.

5. Are there other considerations to help the person in charge get this task done?

Now new agents fill out their bio questionnaires before they even join Echo. This ensures that the questionnaires will be completed before we schedule a film date. Our photojournalist uses a set formula to choose one or two items in the bio script to include in the video, and we give the incoming agents instructions on how to dress ahead of schedule so they're prepared for the video shoot.

Now It's Your Turn!

If you had to leave town for a month, what tasks would you have to delegate? List all of them. All of them. This will be uncomfortable, but remember, you aren't going to be available, so you must delegate tasks. Really think this out. How would you go about it? Now take three of those items and implement a plan to delegate them immediately.

Chapter 12:
Spread the Peanut Butter.
And the Word.

The media interest just kept building. Other press included CBS, which filmed our agent who lived at The Club at Ibis making 2,049 sandwiches with the help of the Club. Then ABC had me on again. Both *The Palm Beach Post* and *TC Palm* in Martin County had us make sandwiches and did a story. *The Palm Beach Post* wanted their own photos and asked us to come back and make the sandwiches specifically for their photo session (this was the fourth round of sandwich-making at the office) and then *TC Palm* filmed women making sandwiches at Willoughby Country Club. FOX also ran our story nationally! Other places where we spread the word were my weekly newsletters and our social media pages.

Our newsletters go out once a week; they highlight open houses and include a real estate article I've written about a relevant topic. That relevant topic became our PB&J sandwiches. Many newsletter recipients got involved and got their communities involved, and in some cases, private companies jumped in. Social media did its thing as well. (Social worked best when we went into our individual subdivision pages.) Later on, we learned how to throw PB&J Jam parties.

See PB&J in the press

The Palm Beach Post | SATURDAY, OCTOBER 22, 2022 | **1B**

LOCAL   + BUSINESS

PB&J FOR IAN VICTIMS

Echo Fine Properties' Miriam Jesselli, left, Adam Andrew Levy, Ana Esposito and founder Jeff Lichtenstein, far right, make peanut butter and jelly sandwiches in Palm Beach Gardens on Friday. The company created Coming Together and Sticking Together that makes and delivers the sandwiches to Hurricane Ian victims.

PHOTOS BY GREG LOVETT/PALM BEACH POST

Palm Beach Post on PB&J Drive

47

NFL Hall of Famer Willie Roaf & Reporter Derek Lowe

From left to right... Reporter Derek Lowe,
Penny Burke, Jeff Lichtenstein

Chapter 13:
Expected Surprises

A few people told me that our office making PB&Js was a great team building exercise. I hadn't exactly expected that, but we were prepared for the unexpected. People shared how to ask for donations. We had to work together about where to put ingredients, how to acquire tables, how to lay out and arrange tables, and how to put out tablecloths. Even learning how to properly spread and apply the PB and jelly was a team experience. Someone suggested using long spoons to get the peanut butter out better since the plastic spoons kept breaking. What to do with the crust and making fun of people who squirted out too much jelly provoked lots of laughter. Laughter became a core part of our collective experience.

People who hadn't met up or been back to the office in years were interacting and having fun with each other.

Ideas were starting to flow, spurring lots of creativity. No matter what people's political beliefs were or what their state of mind was when they'd walked in, the mood was collaborative and joyous. Making PB&J sandwiches was a COVID-breaker in that respect, and the experience led to agent discussions about how we could get more people involved. We also talked about how if we could implement this effort so quickly, how could we later implement projects in our own areas that we'd let go dormant?

We had accidentally (but fortuitously!) taught ourselves that keeping an open mind makes for a better, more effective, and easier product. We were stunned to see how many ways people problem-solved with different and more productive solutions.

In a nutshell, PB&J was revitalizing our people and our business.

Exercise:
Building Company Culture

The documentary *The Last Dance* was about the Chicago Bulls—it covered the period when Michael Jordan was drafted in 1984 until the Bulls won their last championship in 1998. Jordan has said that the Bulls of 1984 were talented individually but dysfunctional as a team. Jerry Krause, the general manager of the Bulls, did addition by subtraction: he traded away selfish players, players with drug-related issues, and players with bad attitudes and then replaced them with role-model players, players with good attitudes, and self-sacrificing, team-oriented players. Krause also drafted talented players who had a team-oriented attitude. Six championships later, the results spoke for themselves.

Whenever a new agent joins Echo, we send out a welcome text introducing the agent to every staff member and anyone who's going to assist them during their training. That makes the agent immediately feel welcome. The agent then cycles through every department: our photojournalist does a personal video of them, our photographer takes lifestyle shots, our administrator goes through any contract questions, and our lead client concierge does one-on-one training with them on our system. The agent is introduced to other agents through small group trainings. Our office is collaborative—anyone will help you, let you sit in their office, and invite you to follow them in the field.

We have a hiring philosophy of "You can't do a good deal with a bad guy." We tell potential hires that if you look to gossip, you won't find anyone here to gossip with. That lets everyone work more closely together and feel free to contact each other. We also have a lot of fun and laugh a lot. That forms a positive basis for the company culture and allows new agents in particular to learn and get things done.

Now It's Your Turn!

Do you have any people in your company who are negative? Can you help them by doing any collaborative activities? Do they just need to be heard?

Identify the negative people in your organization. Be bold and address the situation with them. You can't help solve an issue if you refuse to even acknowledge it.

Come up with a team-oriented event where you all have to do something together. It could be something as simple as working together in a "rage room" (something we did) or putting together a company "pet day" to showcase your teammates' furry friends (something we also did). Whatever it is, make it fun! Laughter will help erode tension.

After the event, come up with a plan to address any difficult behavior if it still exists. If it can't be fixed, are you willing to help that person move on?

Chapter 14:
"It's 5 O'Clock Somewhere"? Not Here, It Ain't.

The historic small town of Matlacha on the way to Pine Island was devastated, almost obliterated. Darling little restaurants, antique stores, and touristy gift and souvenir spots were totally demolished. It seemed like there was a tree lying on top of every home. Power poles had come down like dominos. I witnessed one family dissolve into tears in their driveway—they had a complete breakdown upon getting back home and seeing their house ripped to shreds.

Garbage was piled up sky-high. There was no electricity, and running water was only turned on for two hours each day for fear of the water backing up in the system. And people weren't just affected by the disaster of losing their possessions—multiple signs spelling out "Armed and will shoot!" could be seen in many places. Residents knew a major lifestyle change could be coming.

Once the rebuilding has been completed, older wood-frame construction will likely be replaced by more modern homes.

Developers will be licking their chops to come in since residents won't be allowed to rebuild exactly what was already there (and couldn't afford to do so even if they were able to get permission to rebuild themselves). The sleepy quaint town with the "it's 5 o'clock somewhere" way of life was clearly going to be coming to an end. A separate grieving of that future was felt by all.

Boats washed up ashore

Endless garbage

Semi flipped over by Hurricane Ian

Gladiolus Food Pantry

Home swept out to sea

Palm trees and power lines down create danger

Power lines down everywhere

Chapter 15:
Seeing Is Disbelieving

On Saturday, October 8th, we delivered 1,926 PB&J sandwiches to Florida's West Coast. We knew it was bad there, but people were in more dire straits than we'd imagined.

We made three stops in total. The first stop was the Gladiolus Pantry in Harlem Heights (within Fort Myers). Signs saying "Free food" were plastered along the streets, pointing residents towards the outdoor pantry. It was organized bedlam. When I talked to the administrator, she told me that they needed everything and that our PB&J sandwiches would be distributed the same day.

An overwhelming amount of goods had been dropped off, making our four coolers filled with sandwiches feel small. Still, we knew that each sandwich was going to be a meal for someone. And that made us remember how important our effort was.

The sandwich recipients were locals. Lots of people had not only suffered damage to their homes, but they'd also lost their jobs—many work in the island hotels, and given the storm's impact, now they'd have no income. They thanked us profusely.

We all felt bad about that seeing as *they* were the ones in such desperate need.

On the way to stop #2, we saw tons more "Free food" signs, "Roof tarps" signs, and signs offering tree trimming. Palm trees were snapped in half, power lines were down, electrical cords were dangling, and garbage was strewn everywhere. We even saw an overturned 16-wheeler. I'll never forget those images.

The second delivery we made was to Crosspoint Church in Cape Coral. When we drove up, we saw that the church had donated land that FEMA workers were using as their home base and occupying with little tents. The administrator of the church said the FEMA workers and volunteers were spending a lot of their days cleaning out houses and getting rid of carpeting and other wet materials before the mold set in. The food we were bringing here would be distributed to FEMA workers, line workers, and people from the neighborhood.

The last stop we made was on Pine Island. You needed a pass to get onto the island as there were few police present, only two hours of running water a day, no electricity, and the potential of being looted. We took our remaining coolers filled with sandwiches and went to the island, where we gave the sandwiches to organized labor union volunteers. People had come from as far away as Minnesota and North Dakota and from as nearby as Hialeah, Florida.

Everyone we met on Pine Island was incredibly grateful and appreciative; each sandwich given out was a precious meal.

Seeing is believing, and we witnessed the fact that due to the extensive damage, the amount of private support people needed was overwhelming. Fortunately, some places within Fort Myers did have power and people were able to eat at restaurants. Newer construction had fared better than older buildings.

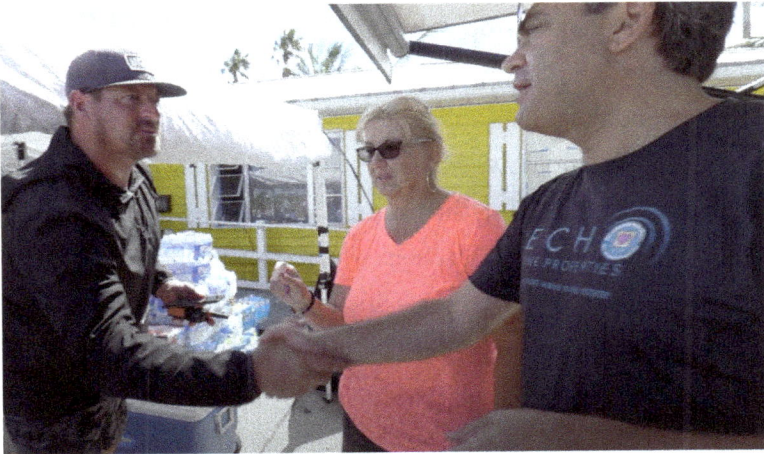

From left to right... Corey Weber, Gaby Hall, Jeff

However, the devastation and the amount of job losses were a huge deal, especially in the areas close to the islands. This was not going to be a two- to three-week cleanup—lots of private help would be needed for many months. In order to demonstrate the urgency of the situation to others in our local area and why help was going to be continuously needed, we included the following message on our blog, in our email blasts, and in our social media campaigns:

We have a lot of pictures and video footage to share with you. Some of these images are distressing, but we feel it's important for all of us to understand the true extent of the devastation that our friends and neighbors in the west have experienced. It's especially important to show those in our local area why help is going to be continuously needed.

The Pine Island stop was at an art gallery called Island Concave Gallery. The sandwiches we dropped off there would go to a lot of essential workers and line workers who were laboring over the destroyed and downed electrical wiring. Lots of volunteers were present, including the Cajun Navy. Some were suspicious and making sure to really check everyone out.

I was talking to the head of the operation when the lady sitting next to him said, "Jeff Lichtenstein! I know you. Do you recognize me?" To my embarrassment, I didn't. She said her name was Gaby Hall.

Gaby Hall was someone who'd done maybe 20 to 30 short-sell processing deals for me back in the Big Short market that ran from 2009 to 2014. I remembered that she lived in Cooper City near Fort Lauderdale. We'd never met and I had always wanted to. Now here we were! The trip and what we were doing took on another degree of added meaning. This was really a crazy coincidence.

A Thank You hug at the Gladiolus Food Pantry

See PB&J Delivery Photos

Chapter 16: Road Rage

I was on such a high coming back from the West Coast! But then when I was about half an hour from home driving along Southern Blvd. and going 70 mph, I was cut off—a driver of a pickup truck purposely swerved close to my car as he was merging in from the right-hand lane.

I thought to myself, "If he knew what we just did—if he knew about all those PB&Js we just dropped off—I bet he wouldn't have cut me off so fast." My next thought was, "That driver should really make a PB&J! Might put him in a better mood."

That's when I realized that PB&Js could save the world.

Chapter 17:
The Temptation
to Deviate

Seeing our initial success made us wonder if we should expand our efforts. Should we start to take along baby formula, too? Bottled water? Pet food? The list of suggestions to change things up with additional items went on and on.

Still, I decided to stick to PB&J sandwiches for two reasons. The first reason was easy: to keep it simple. Our single-concern message was working, and the more we diluted it by talking about other things, the more the power of the message would get watered down. The second reason was that changing what we were bringing would complicate things.

The lesson we learned? Stick to the plan.

Chapter 18: Community Involvement

Once the press had gotten involved, we had spread the word via our database, and our social media messages had gotten sent around, it was time to get individual subdivisions involved in our PB&J efforts. We approached gyms, schools, assisted living facilities, subdivisions, businesses, you name it. You'd be surprised at how many places are looking for things to do together and how many want to help.

Subdivisions were the easiest to get involved. With some, we had to go to a property manager or club manager and pitch our idea. With others, we would rent out a clubhouse or they would give it to us. Sometimes we just posted about our subdivision activity on social media. We also sent out notes and postcards and invited the community to a local pavilion or park where we would make the sandwiches. One agent even held an event in his driveway. All in all, over 20 individual subdivisions or condo developments held PB&J Jam sessions!

See PB&J Special Messages from the Community

Chapter 19:
PB&J Jam!

In total, we had 25 agents conduct their own PB&J Jam sessions. At first, we hit lots of obstacles. Obstacles like "Is this juvenile?" and "How do I do it?" and "What if no one shows up?" and "Is it too late?" Obstacles of simply not knowing what to do.

All of these obstacles are due to fears of the unknown. Interestingly, they're also all fears we have within our own personal lives and business lives. Years ago, I'd found myself not wanting to go to business events because I had put on weight. I didn't want to buy new clothes because my parents had helped buy me my old clothes and I felt bad about not being able to wear them anymore. Eventually, I decided to give myself the gift of purchasing new clothing while working separately on my weight. I got back to dressing professionally and doing more business.

I'll go into detail as to what each of our agents did as extensions of us making PB&Js and getting people in their sales territories to make PB&Js, but keep in mind that besides the connections and branding the agents got from their PB&J Jam sessions, the events also opened pathways that allowed the agents to retool other portions of their business. That was the extended gift of giving.

Jon Hazman transformed his business the most. Jon had only been in the business for a year, and typically it takes a real estate agent three years to really start to gain traction. Part of the reason why is because the agent doesn't have real estate experience. During the agent's first year, everything is new! Learning all the ins and outs of contracts is time-consuming. Just the mechanics of getting into the relevant programs and how to use them—and learning the lingo—takes a lot of repetition.

Homaira Mangal & Layla Mangal
hard at work making PB&Js

Knowing what people can legally do with regards to contracts and understanding all of the related strategies and pitfalls of real estate is overwhelming. At first, agents don't know the lay of the land or the inventory. Agents also don't have an income stream flowing through because they don't have a book of business detailing past relationships. It's been published that the failure rate for new agents is 87% after just a few years.

In addition to all of that, Jon had a fierce competitor who blocked him at every turn. This was discouraging and intimidating (by design) at the same time... yet Jon was the first agent to give a PB&J Jam event a go. I had pitched the idea to everyone in our company, but most agents initially passed because of those pesky internal fears.

I called Jon to talk though the roadblocks. He was in a pickleball group of about 50 people, and we decided to limit pitching to just that group of people. If we brought the idea up to the club directly, we felt like his competitor would find a reason to stop it.

His pickleball group loved it! Jon immediately rented out a room in the Ibis clubhouse. The event hit the social media accounts of his group members, one of whom was part of another group called the Old Geezers. That person talked about it within their group. They felt the same way our group had: they all wanted to do something. They were older, well off, and wanted to help. Once they joined our efforts, a women's charitable group got word of PB&J Jam and wanted to participate.

Word was spreading. Now the news went to the club itself, which sent it out to the entire community. Jon's competitor could do nothing about it—if they did, they'd have egg on their face. All his competitor could do was watch Jon Hazman be the center of giving.

Jon Hazman with 2,000 PB&J's from Ibis Country Club

Ultimately, over 200 members participated and 2,049 sandwiches were made. NY Mets MLB players Lee Mazzilli and Howard Johnson did PSA announcements for Jon. CBS came out and covered it. The club appreciated that—they got added PR for themselves, plus members enjoyed seeing themselves on TV. PB&J Jam was the talk of the club.

Jon met everyone. People came up to him in the dining room and the card room and when he was out for a walk. He was frantically becoming Facebook friends with tons of new members he'd never met before. Afterwards, a postcard thanking the entire community of Ibis for making 2,049 sandwiches (with Jon Hazman front and center) went out to everybody. With just one event of giving, Jon had created what would normally take three years of work.

Another agent, Charlie Gale, had a different dilemma. He didn't have a clubhouse in his community, so he posted about the event on his social media channels within the community he farmed and used the PB&J signs we'd created. Then he went to a community park and set up there.

Dozens came. One person Charlie had met before at an open house saw the sign and wanted to help. When he signed in, he told Charlie he was looking to move and gave him his information. Charlie went through his database and realized that the initial email the man had given to him at the open house the year before was fake. This one was real.

The rewards of giving don't come right away, but they do arrive. A follow-up postcard thanking The Shores for helping make and distribute over 20,000 PB&Js (this time with Charlie Gale front and center) was mailed to the entire community.

In a different community, Dara Dickinson talked to the manager at the townhouse complex where she lived about throwing a PB&J Jam session. The association sent out a notice about the event to everybody, and we also posted about the event on Facebook and Nextdoor and put up physical signs about it. Dara met a ton of people! A follow-up card thanking the residents of Dakota went out.

Dave Peck, an agent and amateur drummer, was actually the person who coined the name "PB&J Jam." He lives in a 240-home exclusive community called Jupiter Inlet Colony (JIC). Dave first approached the JIC Club, which is a separate club on the Intracoastal, about using a room. He was turned down. That was a problem since there was really nowhere else Dave could host the event. The beach was behind his home, but making PB&Js on the beach with lots of sand and sticky peanut butter didn't seem like a good recipe. I said, "How about your house or driveway?" Dave agreed.

But we faced another hurdle: the community didn't have an active Facebook page, which meant that getting the word out would be difficult. We thought about creating a "You're Invited" upscale invitation instead of relying on social media. That could work! We sent out the invitations and created signs.

Now, like I said, JIC is very exclusive. Despite only having 240 residents, it's actually its own town with its own police department. We figured any signs we put up in the community might come right back down since signs weren't really allowed. Then again, seeing as we were hosting a charity event, we thought we might be granted some latitude.

We had 20 people backing us, including the mayor, the social activities chair, and a cop. I put the signs up in front of Dave's house on Friday afternoon, but the commish removed them after getting a complaint. On Saturday, the cop pulled into Dave's driveway and said, "I don't know who called yesterday, but put the signs back and tell whomever has a problem with them to come see Officer Jim." The signs went back up. We had our event!

During the event, a driver in a black Benz took video of us as she drove by. Turned out that she was the one who'd complained. She lived down the street and was a Realtor. Ha!!! So we made friends...and enemies.

In all, Dave—who was also a new agent—made huge inroads with the event. We'd sent out some postcards in his name to give him a couple of layers of branding, and he was also regularly walking through the neighborhood and interacting with people. Still, being new means it's hard to get going. He hadn't sold anything yet and didn't have any listings to leverage against. Selling real estate is like selling in many other industries: when you don't have a track record, it's very much a "chicken and egg" scenario. Which one comes first? Which one can come first?

By hosting a PB&J Jam session, Dave became the center of both attention and controversy. By trying to shut down a giving event, the experienced Realtor damaged her reputation. Dave got the gift of more layers of branding and an additional layer of "good guy by giving." And another follow-up thank-you note to the residents of JIC went out, giving Dave yet another layer of recognition.

YOU ARE INVITED!

Our company (with the help of friends like you) have made, collected, and delivered over 15,000 nutritious sandwiches to those in dire need of food.

I am inviting residents to join us at the PGA National Park (across from Preston) on Saturday November 5th from 11-2pm to make more ready-to-eat, hearty meals.

You need to bring yourself, your family, smiles, and.....
1 Loaf of WonderBread
1 Jar of creamy (no chunky) Peanut Butter
1 Grape Jelly
1 box of Ziploc Bags

Please RSVP to the PGA Team at
Jeff@EchoFineProperties.com 561.346.8383

TO START "SPREADING" WWW.PBJSTICKINGTOGETHER.COM

Exercise:
Always Have Backup Plans

Backup plans need to be treated as planned events. Years ago, a salesman told me something about showing up on time. "You have all night to get to your first appointment," he said. "Plan for traffic. Plan for a train to come." In other words, assume you'll need your backup plan. (And the next time someone tells you

"I would have been on time if a train hadn't come along," try not to roll your eyes.) Have a backup plan in place! Then even if everything does indeed fall apart and the first plan doesn't work out, you'll still achieve your goal.

One crucial aspect of our business is our brochures, which our printer delivers to our office every Friday. What happens if the printer's equipment goes down or there's a missed delivery? That could be a huge problem for us. We've had to map out a course of contingency actions.

- Use a backup printer like Office Depot or Staples.
- Move the delivery to Thursday so as not to be panicked on Friday afternoon.
- Delegate someone to check in all the brochures for each open house we're having on that Sunday.

Now It's Your Turn!

Come up with three things that could go wrong and create a backup plan for each one. Make sure you can carry out all of those plans, especially if any of them involve physical tasks or people being in certain places at certain times. Think about potential problems that could be related to online business activities (like ordering from vendors) and consider administrative needs that could go awry. Come up with backup solutions for each and every one of those scenarios.

Chapter 20:
The Power of Decency

Part of why people do business with certain people is familiarity. Another is decency. Real estate sales are all about both—after all, people are trusting agents with a high-income transaction *and* allowing them into their personal home *and* revealing their personal situation and finances.   Clients look to what agents have given back as an indication of decency.

Dave now has giving back on his record. He also has two more layers of branded mailed pieces that were uniquely about him, and he had the opportunity to interact with potential future clientele. Plus the neighborhood was talking about him! The next time an ad goes by about Dave or Echo, that ad will now be more powerful to JIC residents because they have another layer of familiarity with both Dave and Echo—if someone sees an advertisement with a company or product they're already familiar with, it's more powerful than if they had never heard of that company or product before. This is especially true for real estate, which is why so many people do business with agents they know and are friendly with.

Another agent, Sylvia Meade, took longer to do a PB&J Jam. She lives in a community called Paloma. It's mostly a family community, and Sylvia knew it would be best to hold the event in the clubhouse if she could get it. Sylvia had been with us for less than a year; prior to us, she'd been with another firm but hadn't had much success. However, she has a talent for organizing events.

Once she saw the success other agents were having, she jumped into action. It took two weeks and a lot of political maneuvering, but we got the clubhouse! It's worth noting that lots of agents didn't host an event later on because they were afraid they were too late to the party. But the damage from the storm was ongoing, and Sylvia understood that fact and communicated it well.

The HOA itself sent out two mass email invites. Sylvia then posted about the event on the Facebook community page. Signs went up again. After that, Sylvia just talked it up. Word spread, and she had a great turnout. Like our other participating agents, Sylvia got lots of initial coverage and follow-up coverage and met lots of future possible clients. Branding, networking, follow-up. Giving. So many things occurred here.

Agent Liz Elliott had a unique challenge in doing a PB&J Jam. One of the areas Liz farms, Willoughby Country Club, isn't an area where she's a resident or member. Still, that didn't dissuade her—Liz pitched the event to the membership and they loved it. The club did all of the advertising and marketing for the event.

Not only did Liz get tons of free exposure from the club and meet tons of members and get a follow-up branding card, but our PR company got the *TC Palm* to cover the event and Liz and the members ended up on the front page. The members, the club, the community, Liz, and Echo all got additional (free!) branding and recognition.

Imagine what the cost would be to get on the front page of the paper! Our agents repeatedly had clients receive free emails about an event they were hosting from a trusted source, and they also got free social media exposure from that trusted source. How did they get free event networking? *By taking some risks and doing the act of giving.*

Another one of our agents, Andrew Levy, didn't have a clubhouse to use, so he rented out a public pavilion close to the Jupiter Seaside community that he represents. Invites were sent out, residents showed up, and follow-up postcards went out. The next day, Andrew hosted another event. This one involved The Lord's Place, a local organization that gives shelter to the homeless in Palm Beach County. In a twist, the homeless were helping feed the homeless! CBS also covered Andrew and this story. There's something so right about one set of people in need giving to other people in need. If those who have nothing can give, then we should all give.

Miriam Jesselli, a new agent of ours, did a PB&J Jam in a park within her neighborhood called The Hamptons. She did it with signs, social media, and going door to door with postcard invites. Then we sent out follow-up postcards thanking the neighborhood for their help. Right afterwards, Miriam picked up two listings.

Homie Mangal did multiple things. She did a PB&J Jam in Alton by handing out postcards to the homes she targets and got the use of the clubhouse in her neighborhood. In a new construction neighborhood where she markets, she and her business partner, Robert Heller, did a PB&J Jam by handing out postcards. She also did a session with her school and some private micro groups. All of this resulted in oodles of networking, branding, and follow-up thank-you postcards.

Penny Burke handles BallenIsles Country Club for us, and she did a PB&J Jam in her community. The kitchen at BallenIsles made 250 sandwiches. In addition, Penny was interviewed by NBC at our office when we were making sandwiches. Penny told them a story about her home being destroyed during Hurricane Andrew in Miami in 1991. She remembered how she felt when she found out that food was being distributed and how comforting it was to be taken care of. Several people around town remembered the devastation wrought by Andrew. That interview and Penny giving back is now attached to her resume.

Gabrielle Coutant works for us in Hobe Sound. She reached out to a 55+ community, and they were thrilled to do the event. All by using social media and sending out follow-up cards.

Jonathan's Landing Country Club in Jupiter saw what we were doing and put together a drive all on their own. They physically came to our office to drop off the sandwiches. Getting a chance to meet people in person and having them see our office also helped build branding awareness and familiarity.

Will Dean had maybe the hardest challenge given that there wasn't a clubhouse available in the community he does business in. He had one active listing, but the lady was older and didn't feel comfortable posting about the event on her social media feeds, plus it was getting into late November by then. We had the idea to go outside the community and see if we could get Sandhill Crane (a local public golf course and restaurant) to let us host a party there. We were shunted from one person to the next.

Finally, we ended up talking to the owner, who gave us permission to hold a PB&J Jam at Sandhill Crane. A local mortgage broker we use lived in Bay Hill Estates and was willing to post about the event on social media. We also advertised that we would sign off on any hours kids needed for community service since lots of families resided in the community.

Gathering materials to make sure there was enough backup bread, peanut butter, jelly, knives, spoons, tables, tablecloths, tinfoil, coolers, garbage bags, gloves, etc. was just part of it. Struggling to secure a location, making promotional signs, getting out notecard invites, and finding people to help spread the word on social media was another thing. All of this taught Will to never give up! He'll surely use his PB&J Jam experience to advance his business in plenty of ways. Not only did he meet lots of people and wind up with follow-up thank-you postcards and the event attached to his resume, he made contacts at Sandhill Crane whom he didn't even realize could refer him business in the future.

In my own neighborhood, Howard Freedland and Sophie Schneeberger had a fantastic turnout at Egret Landing. They have a strong social media page, and we found that the best way to promote a giving activity on social media is to post about it and then *interact* with people about it. It's important to reply to questions people ask and then bring up other questions that people have. For example, we would mention that while some people asked if it was okay to bring chunky peanut butter, it's best to stick with creamy PB—while some of us personally like chunky, people with teeth issues need creamy.

The more interactions and more reasons you have to continually post about an event, the better turnout you'll have. We put down 10 signs within the community. Normally, real estate signs aren't allowed, but the community let these stay up for the entire weekend, giving us a good turnout and lots more branding for everyone who drove or walked by. We had nearly 100 people come to the clubhouse or drop off PB&Js! Howard,

Sophie, and Echo owned the weekend with signs, social media posts, and networking.

I stopped by to help as I was coming home from a Halloween party dressed as Charlie Brown from *Peanuts*—I thought it would be memorable to represent peanuts since peanut butter is so involved in PB&Js. We filmed each one of these sessions and took lots of pictures, then posted and reposted everything on social media and tagged all those involved. The pictures were used for the follow-up thank-you postcards we sent out to the entire community. Even people who don't want to get involved like to feel good about where they live.

Personally, I've been farming an area called PGA National for 20 years. Our newsletter attracted PGA National charities to come out to the office while the news crews were present; we also had a number of residents show up to help. In addition, we sent out lots of postcards that resulted in lots of people coming out to a park pavilion we'd reserved. We met tons of new folks and had great interactions and follow-up.

Now, I will say that there were some failures when it came to securing locations. Some agents were traveling; some veteran agents didn't push themselves hard enough. Looking back, there were times I myself should have pushed harder and gotten more agents involved. Sometimes I did make a couple of calls, but a few people have said that I really missed the boat on several occasions, and they're right. In retrospect, I advise this: when you have something this good, have people call their peers, and as a leader, figure out a way to make things happen.

Chapter 21: A 3-Year-Old Can Make a Mean PB&J and 95-Year-Olds Find the Fountain of Youth

When young people see a disaster, there isn't much they can do. They can't jump in like the Cajun Navy and physically help out, nor do they have money to help. What they *do* have is the skill set needed to make a peanut-butter-and-jelly sandwich. Kids are experts at it—most have been eating PB&Js since they were wee little toddlers.

Getting kids involved at any age makes them feel useful... and they *are* useful. Some of them were actually better sandwich-makers than the adults! We had kids as young as three years old help. So did teens: the Jupiter High School Band challenged the Dwyer Palm Beach Gardens Band, and combined, they made over 800 sandwiches. Everybody had a great time. All of this was incredible branding, and again, we met lots of new folks and had great interactions and follow-up.

On the flip side, older people can write a check but often can't physically help much during disasters. However, just like kids, they are excellent at making PB&Js. And something unexpected happens—they're transported back in time and become childlike. The whole experience reminds them of their youth: Mom's love, having lunch with friends, playing in the yard. And it reminds them of giving love to their own kids. We had one assisted living facility belt out over 100 sandwiches and have a great time doing it.

Chapter 22:
The Brady Bunch Meets Reality

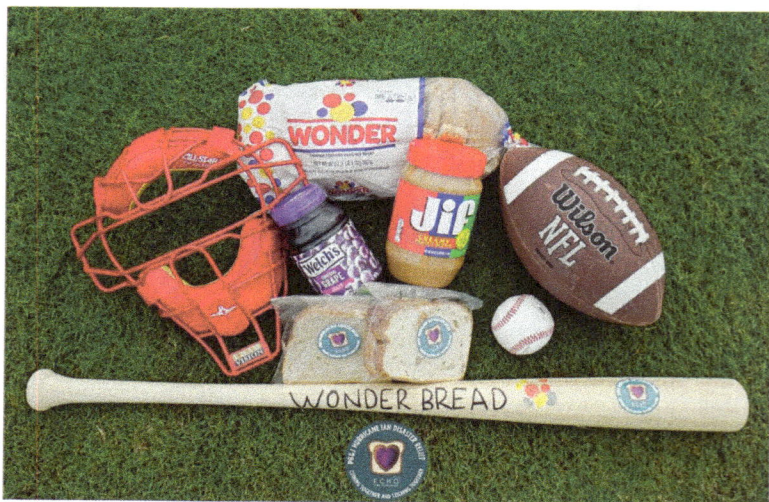

PB&J JOINS the Majors

I knew that Cincinnati Reds MLB Hall of Famer Johnny Bench lives near our office, and being from Chicago and a White Sox fan, I love promotions and wacky things—when I was a kid, I was mesmerized by all the goings on at Comiskey Park, home of the White Sox. Bill Veeck, the owner of the White Sox, was a master of promotions. For example, showers were installed in the stands so the fans could cool off. There was an exploding scoreboard when there was a home run, and organist Nancy Faust played "Nah Nah Nah, Hey Hey Hey Goodbye" whenever the White Sox ran away with the game. Veeck's son came up with Disco Demolition Night: if fans brought $1 and a disco record, they were let in. Then in between the ensuing doubleheader with the Detroit Tigers, radio disc jockey Steve Dahl exploded all of the records in center field. The full house stormed the outfield and crushed all of the records. The White Sox had to forfeit the game. Some say that was the beginning of the end of disco.

Anyhow, I come from those beginnings, so baseball was on my mind and I knew the value of a stunt. I also knew we'd need some additional promotion early on. Who better to catch a jar of peanut butter than Johnny Bench? I had my assistant Phin write him a letter telling him about our good cause, then packed it in a box along with Wonder Bread, a jar of Skippy®, and some Welch's jelly and delivered it. Predictably, there was no response to my moon shot. But a few days later, a text message came through with a 513 area code. 513 is Cincinnati! The text said, "It's Bench. I've been out of town. Mail piled up. Just saw your card."

OMG! Still can't believe he replied. I responded with, "Would love if you were available to stop by our office. Or you could come to Burwick Park and we could throw you a jar of grape jelly and another of peanut butter and a loaf of Wonder Bread and you could catch it to showcase making PB&Js. We need all the help we can get. Very very nice of you to respond!"

I was thrilled to see his reply: "When is a good time? I have a golf tournament tomorrow and early Saturday."

In the meantime, I had realized it would be great if we had another celebrity throw the PB to Johnny. Did we know of any MLB pitchers in the area? But then I had a strange thought: PB and jelly are opposites that go together, so what if we had an NFL quarterback throw to an MLB catcher? I called my PR contact and asked if she had any connection to Joe Namath (he lives nearby). Someone there did know his daughter. The PR contact tried getting a hold of him several times and then said that Joe was traveling and he gets asked to do events for lots of charities. We were turned down, but that didn't mean it was over.

"How about early Sunday or after 12:30 on Sunday?" I texted Johnny. "Would you be open to catching a jar of peanut butter from Joe Namath if he agreed?"

"Sure, 12:30. Where Sunday?"

I got excited. Maybe our long shot could work! "Could we do it at the baseball field on Burns Road? You're probably 10 minutes away. Incredibly nice of you to do this! Not sure if Joe Namath will come or not, but if he doesn't, we'll probably just have one jar of PB and one jar of jelly being thrown. My marketing guy Chuck will come up with a script tomorrow. You're going above and beyond! Happy to do whatever you want to do."

Chuck wrote the script and I went out buy the catching gear. It was Saturday. The first store I tried had closed and moved. Their new location was closed. I raced to Dick's Sporting Goods and bought catching gear, a baseball bat, and a glove. But they didn't have a red face mask, which was the color Johnny wore when he played. I looked for other baseball-oriented stores in the area and luckily found one. It was 4:45 p.m. and I got there just in time. Phew! Mission accomplished.

Then I got a text at 4 a.m. from our PR person: "Sorry for the early text, guys, but Joe is in!!!!" I woke up my wife with my ecstatic screaming. These guys were *legends!* "I'm going to meet Johnny Bench and Joe Namath at the baseball field and we're going to throw peanut butter and jelly to each other!" I yelled. I couldn't help it. Insanity!

As kids, my wife and I had both watched *The Brady Bunch*, and there was an episode where Bobby Brady was made fun of at school because he told his friends he was best friends with Joe Namath. That episode first aired in 1973. Forty-nine years later, Joe comes through again!

At 7 a.m., I called Chuck and asked him to rewrite the script. "Hmm," Chuck said. "Let me think about it—Namath coming in could be the kicker." I immediately said, "NO! He's a quarterback!" Chuck laughed.

We got to the baseball fields early. Our official photojournalist brought one of his photojournalist friends along as backup. We made sure we had three mics and plenty of batteries. At first, we panicked because the fields were locked and there was a farmers' market going on at the time. It was a zoo. But the best field we wanted—the one with artificial grass—wasn't fenced in and it was empty. We were in luck!

A white SUV rolled in. The window rolled down. It was Joe Namath with that Joe Namath smile! "Where do I park?" he asked. We pointed. Bench came in next.

I got out our PB&J t-shirts. Bench put his on. Namath was wearing a flowery Alabama Crimson blue-and-black shirt with University of Alabama logo. He looked at the PB&J shirt. Our photojournalist whispered to me, "It's Broadway Joe—he wears what he wants!"

Chuck gave everyone the script. Bench and Namath are pros who've done a million commercials, so they got the action right away. Like a catcher calling the game and a quarterback barking orders to orchestrate the offense, they ad-libbed the spot easily. There were some fun outtakes along the way when the first jar of peanut butter was thrown high and wide. "Bullpen!" Bench bellowed. "Let's warm up the bullpen!" Namath took the loaf of Wonder Bread and tucked it away like it was a football.

What a magical hour! It was an experience I'll never forget. Athletes sometimes get bad reps, but both of these guys took a Sunday morning out of their schedule and did something nice… and I know that wasn't the first time.

See the PB&J Public Service Announcement

Chapter 23:
5 Days, Then Rest

On the way back from Fort Myers after our very first sandwich drop-off, I had taken a moment to reflect on all we'd done. In just five days, we had created a sophisticated business, albeit to deliver meals rather than make money. In five short days, an idea had been born and developed. We'd had to put exactly the right elements into place to make the PB&J campaign actually *work*. A name, a purpose, a business plan, marketing materials, PR pitches, a website, physical materials, and actual deliveries. All whilst doing our ordinary business. A month ago, if you had asked me how long that would take, I would have said six months to a year. So now why not look at other aspects of our overall business and our individual agents' businesses?

Exercise:
Recognizing Opportunity

Remember Toucan Sam from the Froot Loops® cereal ads? He always said, "Follow your nose! It always knows." Yet despite that advice, most people don't manage to sniff out opportunities.

Echo recently did some sniffing for possibilities. Just like every parent knows that peanut butter has another use—getting bubblegum out of hair—where else could we capitalize with what we already had? For starters, we got into the title insurance business. We knew we'd get lots of that business from our own real estate agents, of course, plus we could also pursue other opportunities.

- Our preferred mortgage lender sends us title business introductions from mortgage opportunities and refinances.
- Our bank conducts transactions with a title insurance company.

Both of these situations involved relationships we already had with people who were right in front of our noses! We just hadn't thought about those possibilities before.

Now It's Your Turn!

Identify a business that's right in front of you, one that you've never looked at in a new light. Maybe it's a vendor you use often who has business connections, perhaps one of your customers is connected to a person or company you could do business with. Maybe something you're already selling could be sold elsewhere. Come up with several categories for these kinds of to-be-reconsidered connections/opportunities.

Chapter 24: Roadblocks & Next Levels

Getting the URL of PBJStickingTogether.com and directing it to our website was a challenge—first we had trouble getting it to redirect properly, and then the email we'd created for it wasn't working. The message tool on the website refused to work. The website graphics were misbehaving and had to be redone.

Past the digital aspects of our campaign, getting a pickup truck to take sandwiches to the other coast wasn't easy. Getting our team to come out and make sandwiches for a second time on a Friday at 4 p.m. and then at 4:30 a.m. on a Tuesday was initially a roadblock. Getting The Club at Ibis to allow us to use their club wasn't easy. We had wanted to host a PB&J Jam at Madison Green, but they blocked it from occurring. Convincing Johnny Bench and Joe Namath to come out and do a spot took several attempts. Asking our agents to host events was initially met with skepticism.

But despite all of that, whenever we found ourselves up against roadblocks, we found new pathways. And when those pathways led to more roadblocks, we found new *alternative* pathways. PB&J Jam events made more people aware of roadblocks and how they could find detours. These realizations have spilled over into other parts of our business and individual agents' businesses and has helped our team reimagine possibilities. We took the lessons we learned from PB&J Jam sessions to other avenues of our business. Each step we imagined and then achieved was another level up.

Exercise:
Overcoming Roadblocks

You cannot be successful if you don't expect challenges! So plan for them and execute solutions to get around them. Barriers are predictable in all walks of life, both on a personal level and in business.

Take one small roadblock you have right now. You may not even realize (yet) that it's an impediment. I'll use myself as an example.

1. Identify a small roadblock in your life. It can be something personal or something business-related.
I don't want to come into the office as much.
2. Why is that *really* a roadblock?
I can't fit into my clothes.
3. Analyze why you aren't solving that problem.
I've gained weight and I no longer have the right clothes to

wear. I want to lose weight, but I don't know the best way to do so.

4. What are realistic solutions?

I'm going to lose weight, but it's not going to happen by tomorrow. I could get new clothes until I've lost that weight and then consider buying new clothes again as a gift for myself when I *do* lose the weight.

5. What are the barriers to achieving those solutions?

- Losing weight is not going to happen right away.
- I don't know the best way to lose weight.
- My closet is filled with old clothes that don't fit and I don't want to have them altered.

6. What are the solutions to those barriers?

- Start a journey to lose weight—figure out how to do it and then take those steps.
- Donate the contents of my closet to charity.
- Buy new clothes.

7. Break down the solutions needed to overcome the obstruction.

- Get over the hurdle of feeling guilty for getting rid of old clothes and get over my sentimental attachments to those clothes.
- Change the small lightbulb in the closet to a white-light LED. That will increase visibility and make it easier to see what's in the closet.

- Find a salesperson/dressing consultant at a store I'm comfortable in who can help me choose an appropriate wardrobe.
- Color-coordinate my clothes.
- Find someone to help me with my diet.
- Find a weight-loss regimen that suits me. (I found one through my doctor, who recommended a simple plan of protein bars for snacks and healthy simple proteins for dinner. I learned that most sauces are made of fats and starches and that I needed to cut out those and certain other foods. Weighing myself every week kept me on track.)

Difficulties and fears both run deep in this example. Recognizing the problem and breaking it down led to all sorts of unexpected detours! But once I went through this process, I got back into the office and in front of people. At the same time, I lost the weight I needed to lose. My reward and gift for myself was buying another round of new, better-fitting clothes and having some of the first round of clothes I'd bought altered.

Now It's Your Turn!

Run though the same exercise with a roadblock of your own. See how many barriers you're facing. After you've done the process once, then expand it: think about five roadblocks you're facing personally and five roadblocks you're facing professionally. You may have many more in front of you, but tackling five of each will be eye-opening and will change your life!

Chapter 25:
The Astonishing Bonus of ROI

In terms of our ROI, we probably spent $25,000 on materials, marketing, renting vehicles, creating t-shirts and stickers, sending mailers, and more. I remember getting a bill for $1,600 for bread and another for $2,500 for t-shirts. Stickers cost us maybe $2,000. We spent probably $1,500 in rental cars and gas and about $10,000 for notecards and postcards.

Some of that was for promotional materials and branding, so it wasn't all just money we gave away. However, we did experience a drain on staff resources, as evinced by the fact that our answer rate for incoming calls slipped from 92% to 80%. Driving three to four hours around town and then three to four hours to the other coast was a full-day affair. There's a real cost to that, including lost productivity.

How many listings and buyers did we land from our efforts? How much brand awareness did we build? I don't know what the cost would have been to have *The Palm Beach Post* put us on the front page of the paper or if such a thing would even be possible.

And what about NBC and FOX covering us, which resulted in us dominating the entire morning news? News coverage is estimated to have a 3:1 value ratio compared to advertisements. Ads are great, but people put greater trust in what they see from an independent organization.

So many connections were made through the PB&J Jam sessions! Some doubtless won't pay off until a decade later. Agents also got woken up and back to work, and there's ROI in that. There's also ROI in recruiting and retention plus in the host of ideas that were born out of our efforts. So what's the potential total value of our exposure? We estimated that between the added marketing opportunities, PR exposure, ability to meet others, and ideas born from PB&J Jam sessions, we'll net a half a million dollars as a return on our investment. And there's considerable value that comes from being seen as an innovator!

Chapter 26:
Branding

PB&J sandwiches are a unique product for several reasons, one being that they have near 100% universal likeability. (It's true that 1.2% of people are allergic to peanut butter—and they know that and stay away—and probably another 1.2% of people just don't like PB&Js.) PB&J sandwiches involve all of the senses. The sight of purple jelly squirting out of a bottle and the spreading of golden peanut butter makes eyes widen. The smell reminds everybody of good childhood memories. The touch of holding a sandwich or cutting it in half is familiar. The taste brings up happy memories.

People from every walk of life joined us at our PB&J Jam sessions: young and old, rich and poor, conservative and liberal. (I recently watched the Ken Burns documentary *The U.S. and the Holocaust.* One of the survivor's first good memories was arriving at Ellis Island and tasting Wonder Bread.) Everyone got involved and had the best time making sandwiches. The good time, the smells, the togetherness, the happiness...all of that was associated with Echo Fine Properties and our real estate agents. Now anyone who participated can't help but think of Echo

Fine Properties when they encounter a peanut-butter-and-jelly sandwich, which for us has become a perfect mnemonic.

Exercise:
The Importance of Branding

Realtors and salespeople often don't think of themselves as being in the branding business, but they sure are! When I first moved to Florida, I went to my job interview in a suit and tie. I *always* wore a suit and tie, even when I made sales calls as I traveled through the US. One of the brokers I interviewed with said, "That's a great look!" He wasn't talking about the specific outfit I was wearing—he was talking about the branding itself when I told him I always wore a suit. I became known as "the real estate agent who always dresses up in a suit." That became part of my brand.

Beyond that, I'll offer you a more specific example of branding in our business.

1. Echo wanted to brand the listing portion of our business. We do a giant laundry list of items that our competition can't match! Conveying and selling all of that with a single thought was not easy.

2. The catalogue of what we do for each client is long because of our setup—since we have our own internal IT staff, photographer, and photojournalist, each listing always gets a number of things, from

night photography to Matterport tours to eight-page brochures. When we added everything up, we had a list of 57 items.

3. We had already gotten some assistance from an advertising firm that had come up with a wordplay advertising campaign called "Home ECHOnomics." It included the home itself and the financials of the home and had our brand name in it.

4. We added the word "guarantee." The "Home ECHOnomics Guarantee" then became a way we could brand what we really do in a way that was memorable for the consumer.

Now It's Your Turn!

1. What's something you do that's different? It could also be something you do extremely well even if competitors are doing it (as long as your competitors haven't branded it).

2. Are any of your competitors advertising that thing that makes you stand out? Years ago, Mobil used having detergent in their gasoline as a selling feature. Other oil companies also used detergent, but by actually advertising it, Mobil owned the "detergent" positioning. Even if a competitor started advertising their detergent additive, Mobil would come to the consumer's mind because they'd gotten there first.

3. Once you spot what you're doing differently, think about whether or not it needs refining, then come up with a tagline involving it. Where else can that tagline go? Someplace where you already advertise? New places? Think bumper stickers, websites, email signatures, brochures...the list goes on and on. The more you consistently use the tagline and get behind it, the more likely the consumer will be to associate the tagline with you and remember you.

Chapter 27:
The PB&J Miracle

My expectation for our PB&J Jam events was that the effort was something we were passionate about, something we could do that was good and would involve the community, and something that would result in positive PR for the company. Little did I know we would get all of that times a thousand!! Although we started out with 20 out of 80 people on the first Zoom call, eventually nearly everyone at our firm pitched in.

All in all, we made and delivered 25,000 PB&J sandwiches. Our organization had an idea and implemented it precisely, quickly, creatively, and collaboratively. We adapted as new opportunities came into sight. We overcame roadblocks and found new paths to get through those roadblocks. We involved our vendors, our clients, our database, other organizations, and charities. Celebrities and the press got involved. We used our marketing savvy to push the envelope in this effort.

From condo communities to churches, schools, and assisted living facilities, the amount of people we met in nonbusiness settings throughout the process of holding PB&J Jam events was incredible! That never would have happened otherwise. We were covered on our local ABC station twice as well as the CBS, NBC, and FOX affiliates. Some out-of-state locations picked up the story. *Yahoo News* took it national. *The Palm Beach Post* and *TC Palm* put us on their front pages.

In addition to truly helping people hard-hit by the hurricane, the PB&J Jam sessions were a pandemic buster—people who'd been stuck at home and isolated came in to make sandwiches. That included our agents. The pandemic was a disaster for lots of them, too, with many no longer coming into work at all. But once the PB&J Jam sessions got started, like magic, our agents were reactivated!

The PB&J Jam campaign spurred joy and happiness that had appeared lost. Creativity, ideas, and collaborating sprang back as our agents got reinvolved with their office communities. They met many people and made many contacts, which will expand their own businesses. They got more opportunities to be involved with other charities. Their names were passed along to others. Some estimates are that people need to see a real estate agent's name 17 times before it gets burnt into their memory. The PB&J Jam campaign was like a nine-layer cake of those 17 in terms of impressions and branding! Careers were hypermarketed, and the ROI will arrive in spades.

The PB&J Jam campaign lit a massive spark and also let us reimagine how we could implement other projects. If we could figure out how to launch our PB&J Jam idea in just one week, what other doable business projects were on the backburner?

What else had we told ourselves we couldn't do in the past that we really *could* do?

We immediately started to hold strategy sessions and reexamine our business plans. The PB&J Jam effort was a charity event meant to help others, certainly, but its biggest gift was actually to us in the form of the activation and motivation that the campaign created. In short, the PB&J Jam sessions turned out to be a kind of miracle!

The metrics on our local ABC affiliate were so strong that we got kicked up to being featured on *Good Morning America*. *GMA* interviewed me for half an hour. (They then booked us for another segment on November 23rd, but we got bumped.) We pitched our events to every brand of peanut butter, every brand of jelly, and the Wonder Bread people. I even connected with some of their PR staff on Twitter and through LinkedIn.

We spent thousands of dollars on ingredients. Grocery stores like our local Publix gave us some free food and the community pitched in. Unfortunately, despite the outreach efforts we'd made to the food manufacturers, none of the brands participated, which I found a bit shocking—I think they missed out on a good cause and some excellent publicity. And we had trouble breaking through to some communities, partly because some of our agents just didn't push past the challenges. However, unless you try to kick the ball, you'll never connect. And we connected a lot!

Peanuts! Charlie Brown & Lucy. Good Grief!
Missed Opportunities

Exercise:
Getting into a Creative Groove

I find that exercising my creativity is just like doing physical workouts—the more I work out, the easier it gets to build muscles and do harder exercises. If muscles aren't worked out, flab sets in. It's the same with my creativity—once I get on a roll, it leads to one idea and then to another. My most creative periods are usually a bloom of mind-opening. I almost need to slow things down!

Some of being creative just involves keeping your eyes open and listening: listening to coworkers, listening to vendors, listening to customers, listening to competitors, listening to the world around you. You can often take things that a competitor is doing in a different market with a different product (even in a different country) and apply the same principles to whatever you're working on. As an example, the "Add to Cart" button on Amazon is gold-colored. You *know* Amazon has tested that concept thoroughly. So why not borrow what you see there and apply it to your own situation? We use a similar gold tone for various calls to action on our website.

Let's look at an example of getting into a creative groove. We know that inquiries about how much a home is worth are valuable sources of information. We already purchase some of these inquiries, but where else can we get them? We've realized that we can often get this kind of information from metaphorical real estate we already have. Links to our company should be everywhere!

- In every one of our email signatures.
- On our website.
- In our mass emails.
- On our brochures via a QR code.
- On our real estate signs.
- On our bumper stickers via a QR code.
- On our school banners via a QR code.

Now It's Your Turn!

Come up with an idea. You might say that's easier said than done, but once you get into a groove, you'll easily be able to repurpose your original idea or come up with where else and how else you can apply it! Just keep some core concepts in mind.

- Keep your eyes peeled.

- Get into a rhythm.

- Listen to your people.

- Listen to clients.

- Look to see how you can apply your idea in various ways.

- What's your bestselling lead source? Where else can you duplicate it?

- Pick an idea and come up with three spin-offs of where and how that idea can evolve into another idea.

Chapter 28:
No One Steals
on a Full Stomach

Sterling Wright, a.k.a. "Mr. 100," helped us make PB&J sandwiches at a food caterer location in Boca Raton. Sterling is a celebrity chef who has been on *Hell's Kitchen* and has cooked for Oprah. He and I were talking about how important the PB&J Jam sessions were and how many people don't have empathy for the homeless outside of disaster situations.

Sterling said to me, "No one steals on a full stomach." I asked what he meant by that. Sterling told me he'd grown up poor and knew from experience that when people are hungry, they get into bad things. Having the basics of food and shelter are key ingredients people need to live better, more productive lives. That comment drove home the point that a simple PB&J was even more powerful than I had imagined.

Chapter 29:
Give. And Get. When You Give, You Get.

Kitson Partners made 650 sandwiches as part of our efforts. (They were featured on *60 Minutes* the week after Hurricane Ian because the new solar community they had developed never lost power.) That happened because their HR director looks for a collaborative charity they can get involved in with each quarter. I got an email from their director that read, "If it's not too late, our corporate office would like to participate and make sandwiches. We're in PBG and can easily make and then drop off the sandwiches by your office." Lots of Kitson's employees live in the Fort Myers area and were affected, so this was a great collaborative giving event to do with them.

Kitson has discovered something critical and has encoded it into their company's cultural DNA: scheduled giving is good for their souls and good for their business. Giving helps them become a better organization, one that's more collaborative, close-knit, and fresh. Seeing their successes and our own has made me realize that all businesses should be reaching out to give back to their communities on a regular basis.

Exercise:
Scheduled Giving

Giving can be scheduled and it *should* be scheduled. Scheduled giving gives your people time to bond no matter how big or small your team is. Scheduled giving is best if it's done quarterly; certainly do it at least twice a year. The reason I say quarterly is because that frequency keeps everyone fresh and closely bonded. If you don't schedule quarterly giving, divisions will grow and your organization could get stale.

In our case, we're looking at long-term options for using PB&J to feed the local unhoused population. We think we can extend what we did with our "Coming together—sticking together" campaign. Maybe we'll do it constantly throughout the entire year and have people volunteer in small cohorts, for example.

That said, team building activities don't need to involve disaster situations. How about cleaning up road litter? We got some low-cost advertising by adopting a road in our area—we got two road signs (one going north and one going south) announcing that we had adopted that stretch. The community also benefits from having a clean road that makes the surroundings more beautiful. Of course, to maintain our end of the bargain, we needed crews to go out and actually clean up the litter.

We let the local press know what we were doing, and fortunately, they liked the idea of covering it as a story. We also got local kids involved, seeing as high schoolers need community service hours. (One of our agents bought an Oscar the Grouch costume to use during the cleanup.) Because we adopted the road, we always own the event in terms of branding. That's an example of a scheduled giving event that has paid off with several additional benefits: community involvement, team building, and press coverage.

Now It's Your Turn!

1. Is there a problem in your local community that you care about, your team cares about, or your customers care about?

2. Make a list of ideas. Choose the most appealing one.

3. Will the idea be easy or difficult to implement?

4. Will it involve the community?

5. Will it reflect on you positively?

6. Write out a game plan regarding what you need to implement the idea. Remember to include a name for the event, promotional materials, marketing strategies, social media campaigns, and press outreach.

7. Make a plan of execution. Who will do what? How can you delegate the associated tasks?

8. What are you waiting for?!?

Chapter 30:
Saving Myself.
And (I Hope) You, Too.

Our PB&J Jam campaign affected me on a deeply personal level. I realized this as I got off the freeway on an exit where there are always panhandlers. My previous attitude had been that if I gave money to them, it was probably going to alcohol or drugs. But that day, I gave the panhandlers some money. I think I've become kinder and more understanding of the hardships of others, having witnessed so much devastation. My empathy has notched up to another level. In short, taking part in the PB&J Jam campaign was good for me as a human being.

I'd done some wacky and successful promotions in the past for charitable causes, like our Tug of War to Stop Cancer event. And when the pandemic first hit, we delivered food to the elderly. Another time, we brought Christmas presents for kids in need to a local school. All of those were likewise excellent campaigns, but none of them had the impact on me that the PB&J Jam campaign did.

Conclusion

The PB&J Jam campaign was the most rewarding and fun thing I've ever experienced in my business life. (Maybe my entire life!) Who knew that simple peanut-butter-and-jelly sandwiches could have such impact and change our world? During the campaign, I had no idea what our sales numbers were, but if anyone asked me how many sandwiches we'd made on any given day, I was sure to know.

We did something helpful, and we did it to the fullest. Over 25,000 meals later, it's still something we can feel proud of, and going forward, we'll consider keeping up our PB&J Jam efforts as an ongoing way to feed the local homeless population. Kids are always looking for charitable hours, and each of our agents can participate during certain times of the year as well.

I think regularly scheduling events is something we simply need to do as a business. *Demanding* that people come into the office is a losing proposition, but asking people to come in and organically give back while having fun encourages them to come in because they want to. The end result is more production, creativity, branding, collaboration, implementation, and ongoing positive results for the bottom line and for all of our reputations.

Giving to others and doing something bigger than ourselves brought a purpose and a common goal to everyone at Echo. And we had *fun* doing all of this!

Giving helped our immediate and long-term business. Giving helped our branding. Giving helped us reimagine the possibilities of so many parts of our jobs. Giving helped us innovate. And giving helped our souls.

Giving Implementation Plan

1. What is one social issue in your community that's a problem you deeply care about?
2. Is there a need other than money that you can involve your firm to help with?
3. Come up with an idea that no one else in your area is doing. Keep it simple.
4. Put together a game plan of what you need to make your campaign happen.
5. Involve your entire company.
6. Put together an outline of how to get your clients and community involved.
7. Get started *now*!

Happy giving!

Complete Set
of Exercises

Exercise:
Foolproofing an Idea

When we embarked upon our PB&J campaign, we knew our idea stood a better chance because we knew that Lou's similar idea was already working. Lou was using it to deal with a pandemic-induced catastrophe, but the fact that there was a partial working blueprint with proven results removed a lot of risk for us. In the same vein, when we wanted to get into commercial real estate and title insurance and when we wanted to expand our footprint into Martin County and Southern Palm Beach County, we had similar had-sort-of-done-it-already advantages.

- Our existing agents had clients who were looking for commercial property.
- Our new residential leads were sometimes also looking for commercial property.
- Both commercial real estate and title insurance were related businesses to what we were already doing.
- Our existing agents oftentimes recommended how to handle title insurance.
- We didn't need to buy office space.

- We were already familiar with working with joint venture partners.
- Our website people had worked on commercial websites before, so we had the knowledge we needed to launch a commercial real estate endeavor.
- Going in, we already knew the players in the industry, which minimized our risk.
- Our agents in Northern Palm Beach Country were already searching for properties, plus we were already generating buyer and seller inquiries.
- We'd won Best Real Estate Brokerage for Palm Beach County and the State of Florida. We could obviously leverage those awards.
- Echo was already a known entity—we popped up high in online rankings for the area and we already had the connections we needed in the press to get extra coverage.
- We already had systems in place internally to handle the new business ventures. That eased the cost of breaking into those businesses.

Now It's Your Turn!

What new endeavor are you thinking of doing? It could be something as simple as launching a new marketing plan or as big as an expanding into a new business area. What will minimize your risks? What risks do you face?

Exercise: Storytelling and Selling Ideas Internally

Selling a campaign or even a new procedure internally isn't easy! Often, fear of what your own team might think of it and their potential backlash will kill good ideas because management doesn't want to deal with the potential negativity.

The first part of selling an idea is relating it to your audience indirectly. You might think that the purpose/outcome would be the most important aspect of the idea, but people often balk when it comes to change, even if there's an obvious solution and being stubborn and not accepting it just makes no sense. Let me share an example from our office.

Lately, we've had a terrible time with internal communications and getting tasks done. We have 80 people in our organization, and oftentimes, one hand doesn't know what the other is doing. Communicating by email wasn't working anymore—our rapid growth meant we couldn't just communicate one-on-one without letting everybody on the team know what we were all doing. (Lots of companies have this issue.) One of our administrators said, "Hey, let's not reinvent the wheel! Let's just start with something easy, something we're already using." That something was a program called Basecamp. A few of us were already using it, but our photographer, videographer, brochure writer, and agents weren't.

I sent out an email to everybody (except for the agents) saying that we were *all* going to use Basecamp. Moans and groans ensued. I then used an indirect story of *why* we needed to use it rather just saying "It's going to benefit us": I gave an example of a restaurant owner taking all of the orders, cooking all of the food, serving all of the food, taking all of the checks, washing all of the dishes, and cleaning everything up. Maybe that works if the restaurant only has a few tables, but as it expands, the restaurant owner would have no chance of succeeding. "That's where we are today," I said. People related to that.

After that, I made some individual calls and listened to each person's fears. Then we made a decision that *yes,* we were going to do this. We started by getting all of our staff on board, including the agents. Our administrator and our IT person were already using Basecamp and had already presented it to the staff. One of the keys was not only using the app but understanding the need to schedule each task, with time-blocking in the morning being the most essential function we needed to utilize. (Basecamp is great for keeping everything in one place.)

Then we talked to everyone about how things were going. At first our photographer was overwhelmed, but once he started talking through things, what had initially looked overwhelming wasn't. Then when I talked to him about another change, he started telling me how Basecamp was already the answer and it was the best thing we'd ever done.

Now It's Your Turn!

1. Name one internal problem within your organization.

2. Do you have a solution? What is it?

3. What resistance to the solution might you encounter?

4. What steps do you need to take to implement the solution?

5. When will you get started?

Exercise:
The Art
of Delegation

People don't know how to delegate and often refuse to try doing it. For many, giving up the simplest of tasks is a challenge. "Nobody does it as well as I do," they say. But that attitude ends up either limiting their income or eventually spurring burnout. A lot of that "Nobody else can do it" mindset stems from control, while some people fear working with others. Mostly, though, people aren't even aware of *what* to delegate or *how* to delegate.

At Echo, we faced a delegation issue when we wanted our agents to put their bios on our website and in our printed material within two weeks of them starting with us. Ditto for the agent bio videos. Our photojournalist Rob Moore was originally tasked with writing their bios, scripting their video bios, and then filming their video bios. The problem was that he got busy and the agents weren't turning in their written questionnaire answers to kick off the overall process. Then the agents got busy with business matters. After six months, we had maybe 20% of the video bios. Nobody ever knew what to say or where to film.

Eventually, though, we overcame this roadblock by delegating tasks. Here's an example of how we did that.

1. Identify something to delegate. It can be something personal or something business-related.

We wanted to get agents' bio write-ups, their profile lifestyle shots, and their profile videos done within four weeks of agents joining Echo.

2. Define the problem.

The agents, photographer, and videographer could never seem to get together.

3. Who can we delegate this issue to?

Sara Morey quarterbacked our onboarding, so it made the most sense to assign her this task since she always had first contact with incoming agents.

4. How can the person assigned to this task get the task done?

Sara created a shared calendar and now just books the dates for everyone. We time-block every Friday as a day to tackle this task. We approached a new builder about holding our photo shoots and video sessions at their models, and they said yes.

5. Are there other considerations to help the person in charge get this task done?

Now new agents fill out their bio questionnaires before they even join Echo. This ensures that the questionnaires will be completed before we schedule a film date. Our photojournalist uses a set formula to choose one or two items in the bio script to include in the video, and we give the incoming agents instructions on how to dress ahead of schedule so they're prepared for the video shoot.

Now It's Your Turn!

If you had to leave town for a month, what tasks would you have to delegate? List all of them. All of them. This will be uncomfortable, but remember, you aren't going to be available, so you must delegate tasks. Really think this out. How would you go about it? Now take three of those items and implement a plan to delegate them immediately.

Exercise: Building Company Culture

The documentary *The Last Dance* was about the Chicago Bulls—it covered the period when Michael Jordan was drafted in 1984 until the Bulls won their last championship in 1998. Jordan has said that the Bulls of 1984 were talented individually but dysfunctional as a team. Jerry Krause, the general manager of the Bulls, did addition by subtraction: he traded away selfish players, players with drug-related issues, and players with bad attitudes and then replaced them with role-model players, players with good attitudes, and self-sacrificing, team-oriented players. Krause also drafted talented players who had a team-oriented attitude. Six championships later, the results spoke for themselves.

Whenever a new agent joins Echo, we send out a welcome text introducing the agent to every staff member and anyone who's going to assist them during their training. That makes the agent immediately feel welcome. The agent then cycles through every department: our photojournalist does a personal video of them, our photographer takes lifestyle shots, our administrator goes through any contract questions, and our lead client concierge does one-on-one training with them on our system.

The agent is introduced to other agents through small group trainings. Our office is collaborative—anyone will help you, let you sit in their office, and invite you to follow them in the field.

We have a hiring philosophy of "You can't do a good deal with a bad guy." We tell potential hires that if you look to gossip, you won't find anyone here to gossip with. That lets everyone work more closely together and feel free to contact each other. We also have a lot of fun and laugh a lot. That forms a positive basis for the company culture and allows new agents in particular to learn and get things done.

Now It's Your Turn!

Do you have any people in your company who are negative? Can you help them by doing any collaborative activities? Do they just need to be heard?

Identify the negative people in your organization. Be bold and address the situation with them. You can't help solve an issue if you refuse to even acknowledge it.

Come up with a team-oriented event where you all have to do something together. It could be something as simple as working together in a "rage room" (something we did) or putting together a company "pet day" to showcase your teammates' furry friends (something we also did). Whatever it is, make it fun! Laughter will help erode tension.

After the event, come up with a plan to address any difficult behavior if it still exists. If it can't be fixed, are you willing to help that person move on?

Exercise:
Always Have
Backup Plans

Backup plans need to be treated as planned events. Years ago, a salesman told me something about showing up on time. "You have all night to get to your first appointment," he said. "Plan for traffic. Plan for a train to come." In other words, assume you'll need your backup plan. (And the next time someone tells you "I would have been on time if a train hadn't come along," try not to roll your eyes.) Have a backup plan in place! Then even if everything does indeed fall apart and the first plan doesn't work out, you'll still achieve your goal.

One crucial aspect of our business is our brochures, which our printer delivers to our office every Friday. What happens if the printer's equipment goes down or there's a missed delivery? That could be a huge problem for us. We've had to map out a course of contingency actions.

- Use a backup printer like Office Depot or Staples.
- Move the delivery to Thursday so as not to be panicked on Friday afternoon.

- Delegate someone to check in all the brochures for each open house we're having on that Sunday.

Now It's Your Turn!

Come up with three things that could go wrong and create a backup plan for each one. Make sure you can carry out all of those plans, especially if any of them involve physical tasks or people being in certain places at certain times. Think about potential problems that could be related to online business activities (like ordering from vendors) and consider administrative needs that could go awry. Come up with backup solutions for each and every one of those scenarios.

Exercise: Recognizing Opportunity

Remember Toucan Sam from the Froot Loops cereal ads? He always said, "Follow your nose! It always knows." Yet despite that advice, most people don't manage to sniff out opportunities.

Echo recently did some sniffing for possibilities and got into the title insurance business. We knew we'd get lots of that business from our own real estate agents, of course, but we could also pursue other opportunities.

- Our preferred mortgage lender sends us title business introductions from mortgage opportunities and refinances.
- Our bank conducts transactions with a title insurance company.

Both of these situations involved relationships we already had with people who were right in front of our noses! We just hadn't thought about those possibilities before.

Now It's Your Turn!

Identify a business that's right in front of you, one that you've never looked at in a new light. Maybe it's a vendor you use often who has business connections, or perhaps one of your customers is connected to someone/a company you could do business with. Maybe something you're already selling could be sold elsewhere. Come up with several categories for these kinds of to-be-reconsidered connections/opportunities.

Exercise: Overcoming Roadblocks

You cannot be successful if you don't expect challenges! So plan for them and execute solutions to get around them. Barriers are predictable in all walks of life, both on a personal level and in business.

Take one small roadblock you have right now. You may not even realize (yet) that it's an impediment. I'll use myself as an example.

1. Identify a small roadblock in your life. It can be something personal or something business-related.

I don't want to come into the office as much.

2. Why is that *really* a roadblock?

I can't fit into my clothes.

3. Analyze why you aren't solving that problem.

I've gained weight and I no longer have the right clothes to wear. I want to lose weight, but I don't know the best way to do so.

4. What are realistic solutions?

I'm going to lose weight, but it's not going to happen by tomorrow. I could get new clothes until I've lost that weight and then consider being buying new clothes again as a gift for myself when I *do* lose the weight.

5. What are the barriers to achieving those solutions?

- Losing weight is not going to happen right away.
- I don't know the best way to lose weight.
- My closet is filled with old clothes that don't fit and I don't want to have them altered.

6. What are the solutions to those barriers?

- Start a journey to lose weight—figure out how to do it and then take those steps.
- Donate the contents of my closet to charity.
- Buy new clothes.

7. Break down the solutions needed to overcome the obstruction.

- Get over the hurdle of feeling guilty for getting rid of old clothes and get over my sentimental attachments to those clothes.
- Change the small lightbulb in the closet to a white-light LED. That will increase visibility and make it easier to see what's in the closet.
- Find a salesperson/dressing consultant at a store I'm comfortable in who can help me choose an appropriate wardrobe.
- Color-coordinate my clothes.

- Find someone to help me with my diet.
- Find a weight-loss regimen that suits me. (I found one through my doctor, who recommended a simple plan of protein bars for snacks and healthy simple proteins for dinner. I learned that most sauces are made of fats and starches and that I needed to cut out those and certain other foods. Weighing myself every week kept me on track.)

Difficulties and fears both run deep in this example. Recognizing the problem and breaking it down led to all sorts of unexpected detours! But once I went through this process, I got back into the office and in front of people. At the same time, I lost the weight I needed to lose. My reward and gift for myself was buying another round of new, better-fitting clothes and having some of the first round of clothes I'd bought altered.

Now It's Your Turn!

Run though the same exercise with a roadblock of your own. See how many barriers you're facing. After you've done the process once, then expand it: think about five roadblocks you're facing personally and five roadblocks you're facing professionally. You may have many more in front of you, but tackling five of each will be eye-opening and will change your life!

Exercise:
The Importance
of Branding

Realtors and salespeople often don't think of themselves as being in the branding business, but they sure are! When I first moved to Florida, I went to my job interview in a suit and tie. I *always* wore a suit and tie, even when I made sales calls as I traveled through the US. One of the brokers I interviewed with said, "That's a great look!" He wasn't talking about the specific outfit I was wearing—he was talking about the branding itself when I told him I always wore a suit. I became known as "the real estate agent who always dresses up in a suit." That became part of my brand.

Beyond that, I'll offer you a more specific example of branding in our business.

1. Echo wanted to brand the listing portion of our business. We do a giant laundry list of items that our competition can't match! Conveying and selling all of that with a single thought was not easy.

2. The catalogue of what we do for each client is long because of our setup—since we have our own internal IT staff, photographer, and photojournalist, each listing always gets a number of things, from night photography to Matterport tours to eight-page brochures. When we added everything up, we had a list of 57 items.

3. We had already gotten some assistance from an advertising firm that had come up with a wordplay advertising campaign called "Home ECHOnomics." It included the home itself and the financials of the home and had our brand name in it.

4. We added the word "guarantee." The "Home ECHOnomics Guarantee" then became a way we could brand what we really do in a way that was memorable for the consumer.

Now It's Your Turn!

1. What's something you do that's different? It could also be something you do extremely well even if competitors are doing it (as long as your competitors haven't branded it).

2. Are any of your competitors advertising that thing that makes you stand out? Years ago, Mobil used having detergent in their gasoline as a selling feature. Other oil companies also used detergent, but by actually advertising it, Mobil owned the "detergent" positioning. Even if a competitor started advertising their detergent additive, Mobil would come to the consumer's mind because they'd gotten there first.

3. Once you spot what you're doing differently, think about whether or not it needs refining, then come up with a tagline involving it. Where else can that tagline go? Someplace where you already advertise? New places? Think bumper stickers, websites, email signatures, brochures...the list goes on and on. The more you consistently use the tagline and get behind it, the more likely the consumer will be to associate the tagline with you and remember you

Exercise: Getting into a Creative Groove

I find that exercising my creativity is just like doing physical workouts—the more I work out, the easier it gets to build muscles and do harder exercises. If muscles aren't worked out, flab sets in. It's the same with my creativity—once I get on a roll, it leads to one idea and then to another. My most creative periods are usually a bloom of mind-opening. I almost need to slow things down!

Some of being creative just involves keeping your eyes open and listening: listening to coworkers, listening to vendors, listening to customers, listening to competitors, listening to the world around you. You can often take things that a competitor is doing in a different market with a different product (even in a different country) and apply the same principles to whatever you're working on. As an example, the "Add to Cart" button on Amazon is gold-colored. You *know* Amazon has tested that concept thoroughly. So why not borrow what you see there and apply it to your own situation? We use a similar gold tone for various calls to action on our website.

Let's look at an example of getting into a creative groove. We know that inquiries about how much a home is worth are valuable sources of information. We already purchase some of these inquiries, but where else can we get them? We've realized that we can often get this kind of information from metaphorical real estate we already have. Links to our company should be everywhere!

- In every one of our email signatures.
- On our website.
- In our mass emails.
- On our brochures via a QR code.
- On our real estate signs.
- On our bumper stickers via a QR code.
- On our school banners via a QR code.

HOW MAKING A SANDWICH CAN CHANGE YOUR WORLD

Now It's Your Turn!

Come up with an idea. You might say that's easier said than done, but once you get into a groove, you'll easily be able to repurpose your original idea or come up with where else and how else you can apply it! Just keep some core concepts in mind.

- Keep your eyes peeled.

- Get into a rhythm.

- Listen to your people.

- Listen to clients.

- Look to see how you can apply your idea in various ways.

- What's your bestselling lead source? Where else can you duplicate it?

Pick an idea and come up with three spin-offs of where and how that idea can evolve into another idea.

Exercise:
Scheduled Giving

Giving can be scheduled and it *should* be scheduled. Scheduled giving gives your people time to bond no matter how big or small your team is. Scheduled giving is best if it's done quarterly; certainly do it at least twice a year. The reason I say quarterly is because that frequency keeps everyone fresh and closely bonded. If you don't schedule quarterly giving, divisions will grow and your organization could get stale.

In our case, we're looking at long-term options for using PB&J to feed the local unhoused population. We think we can extend what we did with our "Coming together—sticking together" campaign. Maybe we'll do it constantly throughout the entire year and have people volunteer in small cohorts, for example.

That said, team building activities don't need to involve disaster situations. How about cleaning up road litter? We got some low-cost advertising by adopting a road in our area—we got two road signs (one going north and one going south) announcing that we had adopted that stretch. The community also benefits from having a clean road that makes the surroundings more beautiful. Of course, to maintain our end of the bargain, we needed crews to go out and actually clean up the litter.

We let the local press know what we were doing, and fortunately, they liked the idea of covering it as a story. We also got local kids involved seeing as high schoolers need community service hours. (One of our agents bought an Oscar the Grouch costume to use during the cleanup.) Because we adopted the road, we always own the event in terms of branding. That's an example of a scheduled giving event that has paid off with several additional benefits: community involvement, team building, and press coverage.

Now It's Your Turn!

- Is there a problem in your local community that you care about, your team cares about, or your customers care about?

- Make a list of ideas. Choose the most appealing one.

- Will the idea be easy or difficult to implement?

- Will it involve the community?

- Will it reflect on you positively?

- Write out a game plan regarding what you need to implement the idea. Remember to include a name for the event, promotional materials, marketing strategies, social media campaigns, and press outreach.

- Make a plan of execution. Who will do what? How can you delegate the associated tasks?

- What are you waiting for?!?

The End

My Thanks

Giving thanks to everyone who helped with our PB&J efforts is like giving one of those Academy Award speeches—you're bound to miss someone. But here goes:

Lou Farrell, who came up with Operation Bread Drop and who has constantly advised me ever since the beginning of the project. He's a godsend for what he has done.

Chuck Schroeder, a *Mad Men* mad man who connected me with Lou and helped with our messaging. Not only is he the best, he's also a great friend.

Chris Toth, who quickly designed the logo, stickers, and t-shirts.

Jeff Lobb, who lent his ear.

Lisa Howard, who made 6,087 edits on the first round of this book!

Sara Morey, Rob Moore, Hollie Ilott, and everyone at Echo who made sandwiches, collaborated, and executed this wacky idea deserve the bulk of my thanks. If they hadn't wanted to do something to help because they're such nice people, no PB&Js would have been made.

Kitson Partners, Potions in Motion with Sterling Wright, Ryan Brown and the Cross Country Mortgage Team, the Jupiter High School band, and the Dwyer High School football team all made hundreds of sandwiches each.

All of the country clubs, neighborhoods, businesses, assisted living facilities, and children who pitched in also deserve accolades.

Emily Pantelides and her PR team helped spread the word, along with *The Palm Beach Post, TC Palm,* and our local ABC, CBS, FOX, and NBC affiliates.

Many thanks as well to Johnny Bench and Joe Namath—both are more than just MVPs in the sports they played.

The individual managers at Publix who gave us bread at no charge without calling corporate for red tape approval.

The Gladiolus Food Pantry, my friend Gaby Hall, and all the churches, food banks, and volunteers on the West Coast who helped with urgency and compassion.

The countless individuals who dropped off everything from brands of peanut butter and jelly we didn't know existed to gas cards for our traveling expenses to coolers for chilling the sandwiches, THANK YOU!

We were able to see some of the recipients, line workers, and families who got to eat our PB&Js. There was no self-pity or "woe is me" attitude—they were thankful to us despite us having so much more. It was a great lesson in humility and a reminder of the way to be.

And of course, I must thank my wife of 27 years, Veronica, who not only collaborated and helped make sandwiches but who was also woken up at 4 a.m. by my excitement...and then later listened to my ridiculous stories about playing PB&J catch with Johnny and Joe.

Mister Rogers once said that when you're feeling down, look to the helpers for inspiration. Well, we found that almost EVERYONE became a helper in our PB&J efforts. I bet the road rager who cut me off on Southern Blvd. would also help out if we met in the right circumstance. We all have a helper inside of us.

My thanks to you for reading *How Making a Sandwich Can Change the World: The Amazing Success of the PB&J Strategy*. If you enjoyed the book, please take a few moments to review it on Amazon. Your review is critical in support of independent authors like myself and for others to find the book. Don't worry, you'll be back to what you were doing in a "Jif®" (PB&J pun intended)!

I'd love to hear from you personally. Share your thoughts on the book and how any "giving" exercises you or your organization have done have impacted you and your business. Email me at Jeff@PBJStrategy.com. Also, check out the website, PBJStrategy.com, and if you know anyone who would benefit from scheduled giving—Spread the Love!

See the PB&J Strategy Website

About the Author

Jeff Lichtenstein originally hails from Chicago. He got his start in the home furnishings textile business, when he was traveling for more than 35 weeks a year selling fabrics. After that business was sold, Jeff moved to Florida and became a real estate agent. Today he's the owner and broker of Echo Fine Properties, a luxury residential brokerage where he manages a nontraditional model of real estate that mimics a traditional business model. Echo has 80 agents, an average of $1 million dollars per transaction, and over $500 million in annual sales. Between traveling for work and making annual family trips to national parks with his wife and two adult children, Jeff has visited 49 states. He's also one of the few Chicago White Sox fans you'll ever meet.

www.ingramcontent.com/pod-product-compliance
Lightning Source LLC
Chambersburg PA
CBHW071418210326

41597CB00020B/3560